HABITUAL BLISS: PROVEN STRATEGIES FOR OVERCOMING NEGATIVITY

"EMBARK ON A TRANSFORMATIVE JOURNEY WITH 'TRANSFORM YOUR LIFE'—UNVEIL PROVEN STRATEGIES FOR POSITIVE HABITS, RESILIENCE, AND SELF-DISCOVERY.

SHAHNAWAZ

Made with ♥ on the Notion Press Platform
www.notionpress.com

"Think of the words in 'Habitual Bliss' like music, celebrating your courage to be happy in every part of life. Picture each chapter as a step, helping you notice the beauty in each moment. This dedication is not just a thank-you; it's saying how much your positive attitude matters.

Hope 'Habitual Bliss' inspires you a lot, making you create a story of always being happy. Your journey is like creating a beautiful picture, and this book cheers for how you make your own happiness. Cheers to living a colorful life, where every day is like painting with happy colors.

Thankful and admiring,

[Your Shanawaz]"

Contents

Contents

Foreword

"Welcome to the transformative journey that is 'Habitual Bliss.' As you embark on this exploration of joy, positivity, and fulfillment, consider these pages as a friendly companion, guiding you toward a life filled with happiness.

In 'Habitual Bliss,' you'll discover practical strategies to infuse your everyday life with positivity. Each chapter is a stepping stone, encouraging you to embrace the beauty that exists in the simplicity of each moment. It is more than just a book; it is an invitation to unlock the secrets of sustained joy and create a canvas of happiness in your life.

The dedication within these pages is a heartfelt acknowledgment of the powerful impact your positive attitude has on your surroundings. Your journey is not merely a series of days; it's an unfolding masterpiece, and 'Habitual Bliss' is here to celebrate the artistry of your own happiness.

May this book inspire you to find boundless joy, encouraging you to weave a story of continuous fulfillment. As you turn each page, envision it as a stroke on the canvas of your life, painting a vibrant and blissful picture.

Wishing you a journey filled with Habitual Bliss,

[Your AUTHOR Shanawaz]

Preface

"Dear Reader,

Welcome to the world of 'Habitual Bliss,' where each page is an invitation to a life filled with positivity, joy, and the art of creating happiness. As you embark on this journey, I want to share the heart and soul behind this book.

'Habitual Bliss' is born from the belief that happiness is not a fleeting moment but a habitual state of being. It's a guide, a friend, and a roadmap to help you cultivate a positive mindset and infuse joy into your daily life. Whether you're seeking to overcome negativity, enhance your well-being, or simply find inspiration for a happier existence, this book is crafted with you in mind.

In these pages, you'll find proven strategies, relatable stories, and practical exercises designed to make positivity a habit. Each chapter is a stepping stone on your path to habitual joy, encouraging you to discover the beauty that exists in even the smallest moments.

As you read, consider this not just a book but a conversation between us—an exploration of the wonderful possibilities that unfold when we choose happiness as a way of life. 'Habitual Bliss' is not about grand gestures but about the everyday choices that lead to a consistently joyful life.

Thank you for joining me on this journey. May this book be a source of inspiration, encouragement, and a gentle reminder that happiness is not just a destination; it's a habit waiting to be embraced.

Wishing you a life filled with Habitual Bliss,

[Your Author Shanawaz]

Acknowledgements

Acknowledgments:

"I extend my deepest gratitude to those whose support, encouragement, and contributions have brought 'Habitual Bliss' to life. Writing this book has been a journey of inspiration, growth, and shared joy, and I am immensely thankful for the following individuals:

To my family, for their unwavering support and understanding during the writing process. Your encouragement fueled my determination to create a book that resonates with positivity and happiness.

To my friends, who stood by me through the highs and lows, offering valuable insights and a shared enthusiasm for the transformative power of positivity.

A special thanks to [MY Father], whose wisdom and guidance enriched the content of 'Habitual Bliss.' Your contributions have added depth and authenticity to the strategies shared in this book.

To the countless individuals who shared their stories and experiences, thank you for being an inspiration. Your resilience and commitment to joy have shaped the heart of 'Habitual Bliss.'

I extend my appreciation to the entire team at [NotionPress], whose dedication and expertise have transformed my words into this tangible creation.

Lastly, to you, dear reader, thank you for embarking on this journey of 'Habitual Bliss.' Your openness to positivity and commitment to happiness are the driving force behind this book.

May 'Habitual Bliss' be a source of joy, inspiration, and a reminder that happiness is both a personal choice and a shared celebration.

With heartfelt thanks,

[Your Shanawaz]"

Prologue

"In the tapestry of life, each thread represents a moment—a choice, an emotion, a lesson. 'Habitual Bliss' is an exploration of these threads, woven together to create a vibrant and joyful existence. As we embark on this journey, let us step beyond the ordinary and delve into the extraordinary possibilities that lie within the everyday.

This book is an invitation to a realm where positivity is not just a fleeting emotion but a habitual state of being. In the following pages, you'll discover the proven strategies, heartfelt stories, and transformative exercises that form the foundation of a consistently joyful life.

As we navigate the chapters, consider this not just a manual but a conversation—a dialogue between the reader and the written word. Together, we'll uncover the beauty of cultivating positive habits, overcoming negativity, and embracing a life filled with Habitual Bliss.

So, let us turn the page and begin this journey, where each moment becomes a brushstroke on the canvas of our lives, painting a picture of happiness and fulfillment.

Welcome to the prologue of 'Habitual Bliss,' where the journey to joy begins."

[Your Shanawaz]

context

" Habitual Bliss. "

Proven Strategies for Overcoming Negativity

Book Chapters

Book Introduction

In "HABITUAL BLISS," we embark on a transformative journey to unlock the secrets of cultivating positive habits while conquering the challenges of negative ones. This comprehensive guide provides readers with ten proven strategies, backed by science and practical wisdom, to empower them in their pursuit of personal development.

The book begins by exploring the fundamental nature of habits and their profound impact on our lives. It delves into the science behind positive habits, shedding light on the neurological processes that shape our behaviors. Readers will gain valuable insights into recognizing and breaking negative patterns that hinder progress.

Each chapter is crafted with precision, offering actionable steps and real-world examples. From setting clear and achievable goals to creating a supportive environment and embracing mindfulness, this book covers every aspect of habit formation. The journey continues with discussions on consistency, overcoming procrastination, and the role of accountability partners.

The latter chapters guide readers through setbacks, transforming mindsets, and incorporating physical activity and nutrition for mental resilience. The power of positive affirmations is explored, providing a powerful tool for self-motivation.

"HABITUAL BLISS" is more than just a book; it's a roadmap for personal transformation. By the end, readers will have a comprehensive toolkit to foster positive habits, overcome negative ones, and navigate the journey of lifelong self-improvement.

CHAPTER ONE

Chapter 1: Understanding the Power of Habits

In the quiet recesses of our daily lives, habits silently shape the contours of our existence. From the mundane to the extraordinary, these ingrained routines guide our actions, molding our character and determining the trajectory of our journey. Understanding the power of habits is not merely an intellectual pursuit but a profound exploration into the essence of human behavior.

- *The Habit Loop: Unraveling the Mechanism*
- *At the core of habit formation lies the habit loop—a neurological pattern consisting of three key components: cue, routine, and reward. This loop, identified by Charles Duhigg in his seminal work "The Power of Habit," is a fundamental mechanism that governs the behaviors etched into our daily lives.*
- *Cue: The Trigger*
- *Every habit begins with a cue, a subtle trigger that sets the habit loop in motion. Cues can be external stimuli, internal emotions, or even specific moments in time. They act as the catalyst, signaling to the brain that it's time to engage in a familiar routine.*
- *Consider the habitual act of scrolling through social media upon waking up. The beep of a notification serves as the cue, prompting the brain to initiate the routine of reaching for the phone. Understanding the cues that initiate habits is the first step toward gaining control over them.*
- *Routine: The Behavior*
- *The routine is the observable behavior—the action taken in response to the cue. It is the habitual script we follow, often unconsciously, in response to the triggers that surround us. Habits, whether positive or negative, are ingrained through repetition of these routines.*

- *In our exploration, let's take the example of a fitness routine. The cue might be a specific time of day, and the routine involves engaging in a workout. As this behavior becomes consistent, it morphs into a habit, fostering physical well-being through repetition.*
- *Reward: The Reinforcement*
- *Crucially, habits are sustained by the reward system embedded within our brains. The reward is the positive outcome or satisfaction derived from completing the routine. It reinforces the habit loop, creating a neurological pathway that strengthens the connection between cue and routine.*
- *In the context of our fitness routine, the reward could be the release of endorphins, the sense of accomplishment, or even the physical changes witnessed over time. Understanding the rewards associated with habits illuminates why certain behaviors persist and others fade away.*
- *Neurological Pathways: Habitual Highways of the Brain*
- *Delving deeper into the science of habits leads us to the intricate network of neurological pathways. As habits become ingrained, the brain adapts, forging well-worn pathways that facilitate the smooth execution of routines. This phenomenon, known as neuroplasticity, underscores the brain's remarkable ability to reorganize itself based on experience.*
- *Imagine these pathways as trails in a dense forest. Initially, the path is overgrown and challenging to navigate. However, with each traversal, the vegetation clears, and the trail becomes well-defined. Similarly, as habits persist, the neurological pathways associated with them become more efficient and automatic.*
- *Understanding the plasticity of the brain is empowering. It signifies that, regardless of age or past behaviors, the brain can adapt and form new pathways. This malleability lays the groundwork for reshaping habits, offering a beacon of hope for those seeking positive change.*
- *Case Studies: Tales of Transformation*
- *To illustrate the power of habit transformation, we embark on a journey through the stories of individuals who have successfully navigated the intricate terrain of behavior change.*
- *Sarah's Triumph Over Procrastination*
- *Sarah, a professional overwhelmed by chronic procrastination, found herself trapped in a cycle of missed deadlines and unfulfilled aspirations. The cue for her habit loop was the anxiety of approaching deadlines, triggering a routine of avoidance.*

- *Through intentional self-reflection, Sarah identified the cues and redefined her routine. Instead of succumbing to procrastination, she adopted a strategy of breaking tasks into smaller, more manageable steps. The reward? A sense of accomplishment with each completed subtask, disrupting the old habit loop and forging a new, productivity-enhancing pathway in her brain.*
-
- *Mark's Journey to Morning Mindfulness*
- *Mark, grappling with stress and anxiety, sought solace in the cultivation of a morning mindfulness routine. His habit loop began with the cue of waking up, triggering a routine of meditation and deep breathing. The reward was a newfound sense of calm and focus that permeated his day.*
- *In Mark's case, the positive reinforcement of reduced stress became a catalyst for habit persistence. As his brain adapted to this routine, the neurological pathways associated with stress response weakened, making room for the serenity of mindfulness to flourish.*
- *The Power of Awareness*
- *Understanding the habit loop and the neurological underpinnings of habits is the first step toward mastery. However, the true power lies in cultivating awareness—conscious recognition of the cues, routines, and rewards that define our habits.*
- *Awareness serves as a flashlight in the darkness of unconscious behavior, illuminating the patterns that govern our lives. As we become attuned to the cues triggering our habits, we gain the ability to intervene consciously, redirecting the course of our routines.*
- *In the chapters that follow, we will delve deeper into specific strategies for cultivating positive habits and breaking free from the shackles of negative ones. The journey toward mastering the mind is an odyssey of self-discovery, and understanding the power of habits is the compass that guides us through uncharted territories.*
- *As we partake in this exploration, let us remain mindful of the profound impact habits wield in our lives. Each cue, routine, and reward are a brushstroke on the canvas of our existence, painting a portrait of who we are and who we aspire to become. In the realm of habits, self-awareness is the artist's brush, and the masterpiece is the life we craft through intentional and purposeful choices.*

CHAPTER TWO

Chapter 2: The Science Behind Positive Habits

As we venture further into the intricate landscape of habit formation, Chapter 2 unravels the scientific tapestry that underlies the cultivation of positive habits. Beyond the realm of anecdotal evidence, we delve into the neurological intricacies and psychological principles that govern the formation of habits. Understanding the science behind positive habits empowers us with the knowledge to sculpt intentional and transformative routines.

The Brain's Reward System: Dopamine and Habitual Bliss

At the heart of positive habit formation lies the brain's reward system, a complex interplay of neurotransmitters that reinforces behaviors. Chief among these neurotransmitters is dopamine, often referred to as the "feel-good" chemical. Dopamine plays a pivotal role in creating the pleasurable sensations associated with rewards, fostering a positive feedback loop.

Dopamine and Positive Reinforcement

When we engage in a behavior with positive outcomes, such as completing a task or achieving a goal, the brain releases dopamine. This surge of dopamine creates a sense of pleasure and satisfaction, linking the associated behavior with a positive experience. In the context of habit formation, understanding the role of dopamine provides a key to unlocking the potential for positive reinforcement.

Consider the habit of regular exercise. The act of working out triggers the release of dopamine, creating a pleasurable sensation. Over time, this positive reinforcement strengthens the habit loop, making it more likely for individuals to adhere to their exercise routine.

Neuroplasticity Revisited: Rewiring for Positivity

Building on the concept introduced in Chapter 1, neuroplasticity is the brain's remarkable ability to adapt and reorganize itself in response to experience. When it comes to positive habit formation, neuroplasticity serves as the sculptor's chisel, shaping new pathways that lead to constructive behaviors.

Repetition and Neural Rewiring

The process of forming positive habits involves the repetition of desired behaviors, leading to the strengthening of neural connections associated with those actions. Just as a path becomes well-worn with frequent use, the neurological pathways linked to positive habits become more efficient and automatic with consistent practice.

Let's consider the habit of daily gratitude journaling. By repetitively engaging in the routine of reflecting on positive aspects of one's life, the associated neural pathways are reinforced. Over time, the brain adapts, making gratitude a more natural and ingrained response.

Breaking Old Habits through Neuroplasticity

Neuroplasticity is not solely about forging new pathways; it also provides the means to break free from the chains of undesirable habits. By consciously redirecting behavior and consistently reinforcing new patterns, individuals can weaken the neural pathways associated with negative habits.

For example, someone aiming to overcome the habit of excessive snacking might consciously replace the routine with a healthier alternative. The more this new behavior is repeated, the more the brain adapts, creating a diversion from the well-established neural pathways of the old habit.

The Role of Habit Cues in Neural Activation

Cues, as explored in Chapter 1, act as triggers for habit loops. In the realm of neuroscience, cues are associated with specific patterns of neural activation. Understanding how cues influence the brain allows us to strategically incorporate them into the design of positive habits.

Neural Encoding of Cues

When a cue is encountered, the brain undergoes a process of neural encoding, registering the stimulus and initiating the habit loop. This encoding involves the activation of specific brain regions associated with attention, memory, and motivation.

In the context of positive habits, intentional cue selection becomes a powerful tool. For instance, if the goal is to establish a daily reading habit, designating a specific time or location as the cue helps encode the behavior in neural circuitry.

Case Studies: Neural Transformations in Action

To further illuminate the science behind positive habits, let's delve into real-world examples showcasing the neurological transformations that accompany intentional habit cultivation.

Lisa's Journey to Mindful Eating

Lisa, struggling with impulsive eating habits, embarked on a journey to cultivate mindful eating practices. The cue for her habit loop was the sensation of hunger, triggering a routine of hasty and unhealthy food choices. Through mindfulness techniques, she consciously redirected her routine, engaging in deliberate and attentive eating.

Neurologically, this shift involved activating regions associated with self-control and conscious decision-making. Over time, as Lisa consistently practiced mindful eating, the neural pathways connected to impulsive behavior weakened. The result was a positive habit loop centered around intentional and nourishing food choices.

James' Quest for Consistent Productivity

James, plagued by a cycle of procrastination, sought to instill a positive work routine. His cue was the start of the workday, triggering a routine of distractions and delays. By implementing the Pomodoro Technique—breaking work into focused intervals—he strategically rewired his neural pathways.

The cue of the workday initiated a routine of intense focus during short intervals, activating brain regions associated with attention and productivity. Over time, James experienced heightened concentration as the neural pathways linked to procrastination diminished.

The Intersection of Mindfulness and Habitual Change

Mindfulness, the practice of being present and fully engaged in the current moment, emerges as a potent catalyst for positive habit formation. The synergy between mindfulness and neuroplasticity offers a unique avenue for reshaping habits.

Mindfulness and Neural Integration

Research suggests that mindfulness practices can lead to changes in brain structure and function. Regular mindfulness meditation has been associated with increased gray matter density in brain regions linked to self-awareness, compassion, and introspection.

For individuals seeking positive habit change, incorporating mindfulness techniques enhances the neural integration of intentional behaviors. By cultivating awareness of the present moment, individuals can consciously shape their responses to habit cues and reinforce positive routines.

Strategies for Leveraging the Science of Positive Habits

Armed with the knowledge of the science behind positive habits, readers are poised to embark on a journey of intentional habit cultivation. Chapter 2 concludes with a collection of strategies grounded in neuroscience and psychology, providing actionable steps for reshaping behaviors.

1. Strategic Cue Selection: Identify specific cues associated with desired habits and strategically incorporate them into daily routines to activate the habit loop consciously.

2. Dopamine-Driven Rewards: Pair positive habits with rewards that trigger dopamine release, reinforcing the pleasurable aspects of the behavior.

3. Consistent Repetition: Recognize the power of repetition in neural rewiring and commit to consistent practice of positive behaviors to strengthen associated pathways.

4. Mindful Integration: Integrate mindfulness practices into daily routines to enhance self-awareness and consciously shape responses to habit cues.

5. Neuroplasticity Exercises: Engage in activities that challenge the brain and promote neuroplasticity, such as learning new skills or exposing oneself to novel experiences.

6. Behavioral Substitution: Replace undesirable habits with positive alternatives, consciously reinforcing new neural pathways while weakening old ones.

7. Visualization Techniques: Utilize the power of mental imagery to visualize successful habit execution, activating neural networks associated with positive outcomes.

In mastering the science behind positive habits, readers equip themselves with a profound understanding of the neurological and psychological processes that underpin behavioral change. As we move forward, the journey toward cultivating positive habits becomes a deliberate and empowered endeavor, guided by the wisdom embedded in the intricate dance of neurons and neurotransmitters.

CHAPTER THREE

Chapter 3: Identifying and Breaking Negative Patterns

In the intricate tapestry of human behavior, negative patterns can emerge as formidable obstacles on the path to personal development. Chapter 3 delves into the crucial process of identifying and breaking these patterns, offering readers a roadmap to liberation from the shackles of counterproductive habits. Through self-awareness, intentional intervention, and the application of proven strategies, individuals can navigate the labyrinth of negative patterns toward a more empowered and fulfilling life.

The Genesis of Negative Patterns

Before embarking on the journey of transformation, it is essential to understand how negative patterns take root. These patterns often originate from a combination of environmental influences, past experiences, and internal beliefs. Identifying the genesis of negative patterns is akin to shining a light into the darkness, revealing the hidden factors that contribute to habitual behaviors.

Environmental Triggers

External factors in our environment can serve as potent triggers for negative patterns. Stressful work environments, toxic relationships, or exposure to unhealthy habits can all contribute to the formation and reinforcement of negative behavioral loops. Understanding these external influences is pivotal in breaking free from the gravitational pull of destructive routines.

Consider the negative pattern of emotional eating. A stressful workplace might act as a cue, triggering the routine of seeking comfort in unhealthy snacks. By recognizing the environmental trigger, individuals can take proactive steps to address the root cause of the behavior.

Emotional and Psychological Roots

Negative patterns often find fertile ground in unaddressed emotions and unresolved psychological issues. Past traumas, low self-esteem, or a lack of coping mechanisms can contribute to the perpetuation of harmful habits. Unraveling the emotional and psychological roots of negative patterns is a transformative step toward breaking free from their grip.

For instance, someone with a habit of excessive procrastination may harbor deep-seated fears of failure. By delving into the emotional landscape, individuals can confront these fears, diminishing the power of procrastination as a coping mechanism.

Self-Reflection: Illuminating the Shadows

The first step in breaking negative patterns is to turn the spotlight inward through intentional self-reflection. This process involves cultivating a heightened awareness of one's thoughts, emotions, and behaviors. Self-reflection serves as a mirror, allowing individuals to examine the intricacies of their internal landscape.

Journaling as a Tool for Self-Reflection

Journaling is a powerful method for facilitating self-reflection. By putting thoughts on paper, individuals externalize their internal dialogue, gaining clarity on patterns that may have eluded conscious awareness. Through consistent journaling, themes and triggers associated with negative habits begin to emerge.

A journal entry might explore the feelings and circumstances surrounding a particular negative pattern, shedding light on the underlying factors contributing to its persistence. Over time, patterns become discernible, laying the foundation for targeted intervention.

The Role of Mindfulness in Self-Reflection

Mindfulness, introduced in Chapter 2, emerges as a crucial ally in the process of self-reflection. By cultivating a non-judgmental awareness of the present moment, individuals can observe their thoughts and emotions without becoming entangled in them. Mindfulness serves as a compass, guiding individuals through the labyrinth of their internal landscape.

For example, in moments of stress that typically trigger negative patterns, practicing mindfulness allows individuals to observe their reactions objectively. This awareness creates a mental space for intentional responses, breaking the automatic chain of habitual behavior.

Cognitive Behavioral Strategies: Restructuring Negative Thought Patterns

Negative patterns often manifest through distorted thought patterns that reinforce counterproductive behaviors. Cognitive-behavioral strategies offer a systematic approach to identifying and restructuring these thoughts, empowering individuals to break free from the cognitive loops that sustain negative habits.

Cognitive Distortions: Unmasking Unhelpful Thinking

Cognitive distortions are irrational and biased thought patterns that contribute to negative emotions and behaviors. Common distortions include catastrophizing, black-and-white thinking, and personalization. By recognizing these distortions, individuals can challenge and reframe unhelpful thoughts.

For instance, someone experiencing social anxiety might engage in catastrophic thinking, envisioning the worst possible outcomes of social interactions. Through cognitive restructuring, they can challenge these thoughts by considering more realistic and balanced perspectives, disrupting the negative pattern.

Behavior Modification Techniques

Behavior modification techniques form a core component of cognitive-behavioral strategies. These techniques involve consciously replacing negative behaviors with positive alternatives, creating new habit loops. Through consistent repetition of positive behaviors, individuals strengthen the neural pathways associated with constructive habits.

Suppose an individual identifies a negative pattern of excessive screen time as a response to stress. A behavior modification approach could involve consciously replacing screen time with a healthier coping mechanism, such as a short walk or deep breathing exercises. Over time, the new behavior becomes ingrained, weakening the grip of the old pattern.

Creating a Supportive Environment

Breaking negative patterns is not a solitary endeavor. The environment in which individuals live and work can either reinforce or hinder the process of habit transformation. Chapter 3 emphasizes the importance of cultivating a supportive environment that nurtures positive change.

Social Influences: Allies in Transformation

Social connections play a significant role in shaping habits. Surrounding oneself with supportive individuals who share similar goals can provide motivation, accountability, and encouragement. Conversely, negative influences can impede progress, making it essential to evaluate and, if necessary, modify social circles.

Consider a person aiming to quit smoking. Joining a support group or seeking the companionship of non-smokers creates a positive environment that reinforces the goal of breaking the smoking habit.

Environmental Design: Shaping Habit-Friendly Spaces

The physical environment can either facilitate or hinder habit change. Environmental cues serve as triggers for habits, making it crucial to design spaces that align with positive intentions. Simple adjustments, such as rearranging workspaces or creating designated areas for specific activities, can influence behavior.

For instance, someone seeking to establish a reading habit might create a cozy reading nook, associating the space with the positive routine of reading. This intentional environmental design reinforces the desired habit loop.

Strategies for Breaking Negative Patterns

As we navigate the complexities of negative patterns, a toolkit of actionable strategies emerges. These strategies, grounded in psychological principles and real-world application, provide readers with practical tools for breaking free from the chains of counterproductive habits.

1. Self-Reflection Practices: Engage in regular journaling and mindfulness exercises to foster self-awareness and uncover underlying patterns.

2. Cognitive Restructuring: Identify and challenge cognitive distortions through conscious examination of thought patterns, replacing unhelpful thoughts with more balanced perspectives.

3. Behavior Modification: Consciously replace negative behaviors with positive alternatives, reinforcing new habit loops through consistent repetition.

4. Social Support: Cultivate supportive relationships with individuals who share similar goals, drawing on the power of encouragement and accountability.

5. Environmental Design: Shape physical spaces to align with positive habits, utilizing environmental cues to trigger desired behaviors.

6. Goal Setting and Tracking: Establish clear and achievable goals for habit change, tracking progress to celebrate successes and identify areas for improvement.

7. Professional Guidance: Seek the support of mental health professionals or coaches with expertise in habit change for personalized guidance and strategies.

Real-Life Success Stories: Triumph Over Negative Patterns

To inspire and reinforce the strategies outlined in Chapter 3, let's explore real-life success stories of individuals who successfully identified and broke free from negative patterns.

Emily's Liberation from Emotional Eating

Emily, grappling with a pattern of emotional eating, embarked on a journey of self-reflection and

CHAPTER FOUR

Chapter 4: Setting Clear and Achievable Goals

As we navigate the terrain of habit change, the compass that guides our journey is the art of setting clear and achievable goals. Chapter 4 delves into the transformative power of goal setting, exploring the psychology behind effective goal establishment and providing readers with a roadmap to sculpting intentions that align with their aspirations. Through a strategic approach to goal setting, individuals can lay the foundation for positive habit formation and embark on a purposeful journey of personal development.

The Psychology of Goal Setting

At its core, goal setting is a psychological contract we make with ourselves—a commitment to a desired outcome and the steps required to achieve it. Understanding the psychological nuances of goal setting is instrumental in crafting objectives that resonate with intrinsic motivation and foster sustained commitment.

Intrinsic vs. Extrinsic Motivation

Intrinsic motivation, the internal drive that emanates from personal satisfaction and fulfillment, is a potent force in sustaining long-term commitment to goals. Goals aligned with intrinsic motivation tap into one's values, passions, and sense of purpose, creating a deeper and more enduring source of motivation.

Contrastingly, extrinsic motivation relies on external rewards or consequences. While effective in the short term, extrinsic motivators may wane in influence over time. A goal set solely for external validation, such as societal expectations or approval, may lack the staying power needed for lasting habit change.

SMART Goals: The Blueprint for Success

The SMART criteria—Specific, Measurable, Achievable, Relevant, and Time-bound—serve as the blueprint for crafting effective goals. By integrating these elements, individuals create a framework that enhances clarity, accountability, and the likelihood of successful goal attainment.

Specific: Clarifying the What and Why

Specific goals provide clarity on what is to be achieved and why it matters. Ambiguity is replaced with precision, creating a mental image of the desired outcome. For instance, the goal "Exercise regularly" transforms into "Complete a 30-minute workout five times a week for improved cardiovascular health."

Measurable: Tracking Progress and Celebrating Success

Measurable goals allow individuals to track progress and celebrate achievements along the way. Quantifiable metrics provide tangible evidence of success and enable adjustments to the approach if needed. "Read more" becomes "Read one book per month," offering a measurable target.

Achievable: Balancing Challenge and Attainability

Achievable goals strike a balance between challenge and attainability. While goals should stretch individuals beyond their comfort zones, they must remain within the realm of feasibility. Setting an achievable goal fosters a sense of competence and bolsters confidence in the ability to succeed.

An example of transforming a vague goal into an achievable one is changing "Improve time management" to "Implement a time-blocking system to prioritize tasks and increase productivity."

Relevant: Aligning with Values and Aspirations

Relevant goals align with personal values and aspirations. The relevance of a goal ties back to intrinsic motivation, ensuring that the pursuit resonates with the individual's larger vision for their life. A goal aligned with personal values is more likely to foster sustained commitment.

For instance, transforming "Learn a new skill" into "Enroll in an online coding course to advance career goals" enhances the relevance of the goal within the broader context of personal and professional aspirations.

Time-bound: Establishing a Clear Timeline

Time-bound goals introduce a sense of urgency and commitment. By establishing clear timelines, individuals create a structured framework for their endeavors. A goal like "Start a blog" gains specificity and motivation when transformed into "Launch a personal blog with at least two posts per week within the next three months."

Long-Term Goals vs. Short-Term Objectives

In the realm of habit change, understanding the interplay between long-term goals and short-term objectives is pivotal. Long-term goals provide a destination—a vision of the desired outcome—while short-term objectives serve as the steppingstones that lead toward that destination.

Long-Term Goals: The North Star

Long-term goals encapsulate the overarching vision for personal development. These are often broader and more comprehensive, representing the ultimate aspirations an individual seeks to realize. Examples include "Achieve a healthy work-life balance," or "Cultivate a positive mindset."

Short-Term Objectives: The Building Blocks

Short-term objectives are the actionable steps that propel individuals toward their long-term goals. These objectives are more tangible and time-specific, serving as the building blocks of habit change. For instance, short-term objectives associated with the long-term goal of achieving a healthy work-life balance could include "Establish a daily mindfulness routine" or "Prioritize and delegate tasks effectively."

The Power of Implementation Intentions

Implementation intentions, a concept rooted in psychological research, involve specifying when, where, and how a behavior will be enacted. By detailing the specific circumstances surrounding goal-related actions, individuals enhance their ability to translate intentions into actions.

Formulation of Implementation Intentions

Instead of a generic goal like "Exercise regularly," an implementation intention could be, "I will exercise for 30 minutes at the gym every Monday, Wednesday, and Friday after work." This specificity provides a clear roadmap for action, reducing the gap between intention and execution.

Psychological Impact of Implementation Intentions

Research suggests that the formulation of implementation intentions positively impacts goal attainment. By mentally pre-planning the execution of a behavior, individuals activate specific cues and responses in their brain, facilitating the automatic initiation of the intended action.

Goal Setting and Positive Habit Formation

Effective goal setting is intricately linked to the formation of positive habits. The process of setting, pursuing, and achieving goals influences the development of routines and behaviors that contribute to personal growth. As individuals embark on the journey of habit change, goals serve as catalysts for intentional transformation.

Habit-Goal Feedback Loop

A symbiotic relationship exists between habits and goals—a feedback loop that fuels continuous improvement. Positive habits contribute to goal attainment, while achieving goals reinforces the establishment of positive habits. For example, the goal of running a marathon is facilitated by the positive habit of consistent training.

Goals as Milestones in Habit Formation

Goals function as milestones in the larger landscape of habit formation. Each goal achieved represents a marker of progress, signaling the development of positive habits along the way. The attainment of a goal becomes a testament to the commitment and resilience cultivated through habitual behaviors.

Case Studies: Goal-Setting Triumphs

To illustrate the transformative power of goal setting, let's explore real-life case studies of individuals who successfully utilized goal-setting principles in their journey of habit change.

Maria's Health and Fitness Transformation

Maria, aiming to improve her overall health and fitness, set a specific, measurable, and achievable goal: "Complete a 5K run within the next three months." Her time-bound goal incorporated a training plan and regular progress assessments.

By breaking down her long-term goal into short-term objectives—such as running specific distances each week and gradually increasing intensity—Maria established a sustainable routine. Her consistent efforts culminated in the successful completion of the 5K run, marking not only the achievement of a goal but the formation of a positive running habit.

Alex's Career Advancement Milestone

Alex aspired to advance his career and set a SMART goal: "Acquire a relevant professional certification within six months." This goal served as the North Star for his broader career development plan. To achieve this, Alex created short-term objectives, including a study schedule and practice exams.

Through focused and consistent effort, Alex attained the certification within the specified timeframe. This achievement not only propelled his

CHAPTER FIVE

Chapter 5: Building Consistency Through Positive Reinforcement

In the intricate dance of habit formation, the role of positive reinforcement emerges as a powerful force. Chapter 5 explores the art of building consistency through positive reinforcement, unraveling the psychology behind reward systems and offering practical strategies for infusing joy and motivation into the journey of habit change. By understanding the mechanisms of positive reinforcement, individuals can cultivate habits that endure through the ebbs and flows of daily life.

The Science of Positive Reinforcement

Positive reinforcement operates on the principle that behaviors followed by positive consequences are more likely to be repeated. This fundamental concept, rooted in behavioral psychology, underpins the formation and sustainability of habits. Understanding the science of positive reinforcement equips individuals with the tools to shape their behaviors intentionally.

Dopamine's Role in Positive Reinforcement

At the heart of positive reinforcement is dopamine, the neurotransmitter associated with pleasure and reward. When the brain experiences a positive event or outcome, it releases dopamine, creating a sense of satisfaction and pleasure. This surge of dopamine reinforces the behavior that led to the positive outcome, strengthening the neural pathways associated with the habit.

Consider the act of completing a challenging workout. The feeling of accomplishment triggers the release of dopamine, creating a positive association with the exercise routine. Over time, this positive reinforcement contributes to the endurance of the habit.

Designing Reward Systems for Habit Change

Effective positive reinforcement involves designing reward systems that resonate with individual preferences and values. By tailoring rewards to align with intrinsic motivation, individuals can enhance the impact of positive reinforcement on habit formation.

Intrinsic vs. Extrinsic Rewards

Intrinsic rewards originate from within, deriving satisfaction and fulfillment directly from the behavior itself. Extrinsic rewards, on the other hand, come from external sources, such as recognition, praise, or tangible items. While both types of rewards can be effective, intrinsic rewards often have a more enduring impact on habit sustainability.

For example, someone establishing a reading habit may find intrinsic reward in the joy of exploring new worlds and ideas. While external validation or praise for completing a book represents an extrinsic reward, the intrinsic satisfaction derived from the act of reading serves as a more potent and lasting reinforcement.

The Power of Celebrating Small Wins

Celebrating small wins is a cornerstone of positive reinforcement. Acknowledging and celebrating incremental progress creates a positive feedback loop, motivating individuals to continue their efforts. Small wins serve as building blocks, contributing to a sense of competence and reinforcing the belief that change is achievable.

Recognizing and Acknowledging Progress

The act of recognition is a fundamental aspect of celebrating small wins. This involves consciously acknowledging and appreciating the efforts invested in habit change. Whether through self-reflection, journaling, or sharing achievements with a supportive community, recognizing progress fuels a positive mindset.

For instance, someone striving to develop a daily meditation habit can celebrate a small win by acknowledging the consistency of practicing mindfulness for a consecutive number of days. This recognition reinforces the commitment to the habit.

The Momentum of Small Wins

Small wins generate momentum, propelling individuals forward on their journey of habit change. As habits begin to take root, the positive reinforcement from celebrating small victories contributes to a sense of self-efficacy—the belief in one's ability to effect change. This self-efficacy, in turn, becomes a potent catalyst for sustained effort and perseverance.

Personalizing Rewards for Effective Reinforcement

The effectiveness of positive reinforcement lies in its personalization. What serves as a meaningful reward varies from person to person. Understanding individual preferences and values is instrumental in tailoring rewards that resonate on a deep and personal level.

Identifying Intrinsic Motivators

Intrinsic motivators, aligned with personal values and interests, form the foundation of effective positive reinforcement. Reflecting on what brings joy, satisfaction, or a sense of accomplishment helps identify intrinsic rewards. For someone aiming to cultivate a writing habit, intrinsic motivators could include the joy of self-expression, the satisfaction of completing a piece, or the sense of personal fulfillment.

Extrinsically Rewarding Milestones

Extrinsic rewards, while secondary to intrinsic motivators, can serve as meaningful reinforcements, especially for milestone achievements. These rewards can take various forms, such as treating oneself to a favorite activity, indulging in a special treat, or acquiring a small item of interest. The key is to ensure that extrinsic rewards complement intrinsic motivations and do not overshadow the internal satisfaction derived from the habit.

The Art of Behavioral Reinforcement

Behavioral reinforcement involves intentionally structuring the environment to support and reinforce desired habits. By designing cues, triggers, and consequences, individuals can create a behavioral ecosystem that promotes consistency and positive reinforcement.

Cue Integration for Habit Activation

Cues act as triggers for habit activation. Intentionally integrating cues into the environment helps initiate the habit loop. Whether it's setting a specific time, creating a visual reminder, or associating the habit with an existing routine, the strategic use of cues streamlines the activation of habits.

For example, someone aiming to establish a daily gratitude journaling habit may integrate the cue of leaving a journal by the bedside. The sight of the journal in the morning serves as a cue, prompting the initiation of the routine.

Consistency in Routine and Environment

Consistency in routine and environment reinforces habit formation. Establishing a consistent time and space for habit execution creates a sense of predictability, facilitating the habit loop. Whether it's designating a specific workout area, creating a dedicated workspace, or adhering to a consistent schedule, a stable environment reinforces the regularity of habits.

Consider someone striving to develop a consistent bedtime routine. By maintaining a consistent pre-sleep ritual, such as reading for 20 minutes before turning off the lights, the individual establishes a behavioral routine that signals the brain that it's time to wind down.

Consequences and Outcome Evaluation

Positive consequences contribute to the reinforcement of habits. Consequences can be both intrinsic, such as the satisfaction derived from completing a task, and extrinsic, such as the tangible benefits resulting from habit adherence. Regularly evaluating the outcomes of habit performance reinforces the connection between actions and positive consequences.

For instance, someone committed to a daily exercise routine may experience intrinsic consequences such as improved mood and energy levels. Additionally, extrinsic consequences, such as physical fitness improvements, serve as tangible reinforcements for the habit.

Real-Life Success Stories: Triumphs through Positive Reinforcement

To illustrate the transformative impact of positive reinforcement, let's explore real-life success stories of individuals who embraced and leveraged positive reinforcement in their habit change journeys.

Sarah's Journey to a Healthier Lifestyle

Sarah, desiring a healthier lifestyle, embarked on a journey of positive habit change. She integrated the cue of placing her workout clothes near her bed, creating a visual reminder in the morning. Sarah celebrated small wins by recognizing each completed workout, acknowledging the effort invested.

In addition to intrinsic rewards, Sarah implemented extrinsic reinforcements by treating herself to a relaxing bath after reaching specific fitness milestones. This combination of intrinsic joy in physical activity and extrinsic rewards contributed to the sustainability of her exercise habit.

John's Transformation through Professional Growth

John aspired to advance his career and embraced positive reinforcement in his habit change strategy. Recognizing the importance of consistency, he established a dedicated workspace at home, signaling the start of focused work sessions. John celebrated small wins by acknowledging completed tasks and setting aside time for self-reflection.

For extrinsic reinforcement, John established a reward system tied to career milestones. Completing a challenging project or acquiring a new skill warranted a small celebration, creating a sense of accomplishment and motivation for continued growth.

Strategies for Effective Positive Reinforcement

Armed with an understanding of the science and art of positive reinforcement, individuals can implement strategies that enhance the consistency and endurance of their habits. The following strategies provide a roadmap for effective positive reinforcement:

1. Small Wins Celebration: Acknowledge and celebrate small victories, reinforcing the positive aspects of habit adherence.

2. Intrinsic Motivation Focus: Emphasize intrinsic motivators that align with personal values and bring joy or satisfaction.

3. Personalized Rewards: Tailor extrinsic rewards to individual preferences, ensuring they complement intrinsic motivations.

4. Consistent Routine and Environment: Establish a consistent routine and environment to provide stability and reinforce habit formation.

5. Cue Integration: Strategically integrate cues into the environment to prompt the initiation of habit loops.

6. Consequence Evaluation: Regularly evaluate the consequences of habit performance, both intrinsic and extrinsic, to reinforce the connection between actions and outcomes.

7. Behavioral Reinforcement: Design the environment to support habits, incorporating cues, consistent routines, and positive consequences.

8. Adaptive Reinforcement: Adjust and adapt reinforcement strategies based on individual progress and changing circumstances.

9. Community Engagement: Share successes and challenges with a supportive community, leveraging social reinforcement.

10. Mindful Reflection: Engage in mindful reflection on the journey, cultivating self-awareness and reinforcing the commitment to positive habits.

By weaving these strategies into the fabric of habit change, individuals create a tapestry of positive reinforcement that sustains their efforts and propels them toward lasting transformation. As we conclude Chapter 5, the journey of habit formation becomes not just a destination, but a joyous expedition guided by the gentle nudges of positive reinforcement.

CHAPTER SIX

Chapter 6: Overcoming Setbacks and Nurturing Resilience in Habit Formation

In the labyrinth of habit formation, setbacks are not detours but integral parts of the journey. Chapter 6 explores the art of overcoming setbacks and nurturing resilience—a crucial skill set for anyone committed to positive habit change. By understanding the common challenges, developing a resilient mindset, and implementing adaptive strategies, individuals can navigate setbacks with grace, fortitude, and an unwavering commitment to their transformative goals.

The Nature of Setbacks in Habit Formation

Setbacks are an inherent part of the habit formation process, stemming from various sources, both internal and external. Recognizing the nature of setbacks is the first step in building resilience and ensuring that temporary obstacles do not derail long-term progress.

Internal Challenges

Internal challenges involve factors within an individual's control, such as fluctuating motivation, competing priorities, or moments of self-doubt. These challenges often arise from shifts in mindset, emotional states, or changes in personal circumstances.

For example, an individual striving to establish a daily meditation habit may encounter internal challenges when faced with increased work stress, leading to a decline in motivation or focus.

External Influences

External influences encompass factors beyond an individual's direct control, including unexpected events, environmental changes, or external pressures. These influences can disrupt routines and introduce challenges that require adaptability.

Consider someone aiming to maintain a consistent workout routine. An external challenge, such as unexpected work commitments or family emergencies, may disrupt the planned exercise schedule.

Understanding the Psychology of Setbacks

The psychology of setbacks involves exploring the emotional and cognitive responses to challenges. By delving into the underlying psychological processes, individuals can develop a nuanced understanding of setbacks and cultivate resilience in the face of adversity.

Emotional Responses to Setbacks

Setbacks often evoke a range of emotions, including frustration, disappointment, and self-criticism. Understanding and acknowledging these emotional responses is a critical aspect of resilience. It's essential to recognize that experiencing setbacks is a natural part of the learning and growth process.

For instance, someone facing a setback in a goal to reduce screen time may feel frustrated after a day of increased digital consumption. Acknowledging and processing this frustration without self-judgment is an essential step in fostering emotional resilience.

Cognitive Appraisal of Setbacks

Cognitive appraisal involves the evaluation of setbacks through thoughts and interpretations. Individuals may engage in self-talk that influences their perception of setbacks. Shifting from a mindset of defeat to one of learning and growth is key to building cognitive resilience.

An individual encountering a setback in a writing habit, such as missing a planned session, might initially perceive it as a failure. By reframing the setback as an opportunity to understand underlying challenges and adjust the approach, cognitive resilience is enhanced.

Cultivating Resilience: A Mindset Shift

Resilience is not merely the ability to bounce back from setbacks but also the capacity to adapt, learn, and grow stronger in the face of challenges. Chapter 6 explores the mindset shift necessary for cultivating resilience and embracing setbacks as integral components of the habit change journey.

Embracing a Growth Mindset

A growth mindset, as coined by psychologist Carol Dweck, involves viewing challenges as opportunities for growth rather than insurmountable obstacles. Individuals with a growth mindset perceive setbacks as valuable lessons that contribute to their development.

For instance, someone encountering a setback in a goal to practice daily gratitude may view it as an opportunity to explore new strategies for integrating gratitude into their routine, fostering a growth-oriented perspective.

Reframing Setbacks as Learning Moments

Setbacks provide invaluable insights into the intricacies of habit formation. Reframing setbacks as learning moments involves extracting lessons from challenges, understanding triggers, and identifying areas for adjustment.

An individual striving to establish a consistent reading habit may face setbacks due to time constraints. Instead of viewing it as a failure, they can see it as a lesson in time management, prompting them to reassess priorities and schedule reading sessions more effectively.

Adopting a Solution-Focused Approach

Resilient individuals adopt a solution-focused approach when confronted with setbacks. Instead of dwelling on the problem, they channel their energy into identifying practical solutions and adapting their strategies.

Consider someone aiming to reduce procrastination. Faced with a setback of delaying a project, a solution-focused approach involves analyzing the factors contributing to procrastination and implementing concrete steps, such as breaking down tasks into smaller, manageable segments.

Strategies for Overcoming Setbacks and Nurturing Resilience

Equipped with a resilient mindset, individuals can implement adaptive strategies to overcome setbacks and propel themselves forward on the path of habit formation. The following strategies offer a comprehensive guide for navigating challenges and building resilience:

1. Self-Compassion Practices: Cultivate self-compassion by treating oneself with kindness and understanding during setbacks. Replace self-criticism with self-encouragement and acknowledge that setbacks are part of the growth process.

2. Reflective Analysis: Conduct a reflective analysis of setbacks to gain insights into underlying factors. Ask questions such as, "What triggered the setback?" and "What can I learn from this experience?" Use the answers to adjust strategies and enhance future resilience.

3. Adaptive Goal Adjustments: Embrace the flexibility to adjust goals when necessary. If setbacks reveal unrealistic expectations or unforeseen challenges, modify goals to align with current circumstances while maintaining a focus on long-term aspirations.

4. Mindfulness Practices: Integrate mindfulness practices to stay present and non-judgmentally aware of setbacks. Mindfulness fosters emotional regulation, allowing individuals to navigate challenges with a calm and centered approach.

5. Community Support: Seek support from a community or accountability partner. Sharing setbacks with others creates a sense of shared experience and provides encouragement, guidance, and collective problem-solving.

6. Strategic Planning for Setbacks: Anticipate potential setbacks and develop contingency plans. By pre-planning responses to common challenges, individuals can navigate setbacks with resilience and maintain forward momentum.

7. Celebrating Progress: Celebrate progress, even in the face of setbacks. Acknowledge the steps taken and achievements attained, reinforcing the positive aspects of the habit change journey.

8. Positive Visualization: Engage in positive visualization by envisioning success and overcoming challenges. Visualization cultivates a positive mindset, reinforcing the belief that setbacks are temporary hurdles on the path to success.

9. Affirmations for Resilience: Incorporate affirmations that nurture resilience. Phrases such as "I embrace challenges as opportunities for growth" and "I am resilient in the face of setbacks" reinforce a mindset focused on learning and development.

10. Adopting a Long-Term Perspective: Maintain a long-term perspective on habit change. Setbacks are momentary, and the journey involves peaks and valleys. Embracing the overarching vision provides motivation and resilience during challenging times.

Real-Life Stories of Resilience and Triumph

To illustrate the transformative power of resilience in habit formation, let's explore real-life stories of individuals who faced setbacks with fortitude and emerged stronger on their journeys.

Maya's Commitment to Daily Meditation

Maya embarked on a journey to incorporate daily meditation into her routine. Initially, she encountered setbacks due to fluctuating work demands and emotional stress. Instead of abandoning the practice, Maya embraced a growth mindset.

Reflecting on setbacks, Maya identified triggers and adjusted her meditation schedule to align with more feasible times. She sought support from an online meditation community, sharing her challenges and learning from others. Through adaptive strategies and a resilient mindset, Maya not only overcame setbacks but deepened her meditation practice, ultimately achieving her goal of daily mindfulness.

Jake's Resilience in Fitness Transformation

Jake's goal was to transform his fitness habits by incorporating regular exercise. Despite initial enthusiasm, Jake faced setbacks due to work-related travel and unexpected family obligations. Rather than succumbing to frustration, Jake adopted a solution-focused approach.

Jake strategically planned for setbacks by researching workout options during travel and creating adaptable routines. He engaged in reflective analysis after setbacks, adjusting his workout schedule to accommodate family commitments. Jake's resilience not only sustained his fitness journey but inspired those around him to navigate challenges with a positive and adaptable mindset.

The Ongoing Journey: Resilience as a Lifelong Companion

As Chapter 6 concludes, it becomes evident that setbacks are not roadblocks but steppingstones in the journey of habit formation. Nurturing resilience is an ongoing process—one that involves continuous learning, adaptation, and a steadfast commitment to personal growth. By embracing setbacks with an open heart and a resilient mindset, individuals transform challenges into opportunities, ensuring that the tapestry of their habits reflects not only the peaks of success but the resilience that weaves through every thread.

CHAPTER SEVEN

Chapter 7: The Art of Adaptive Planning: Navigating Change in Habit Formation

In the ever-evolving landscape of life, change is the only constant. Chapter 7 delves into the art of adaptive planning—an indispensable skill for individuals committed to positive habit formation. As we explore the dynamic interplay between habits and the fluidity of circumstances, this chapter provides insights, strategies, and real-life examples to guide readers in crafting resilient and flexible plans that stand the test of time.

The Dynamic Nature of Life

Life is a dynamic tapestry woven with threads of unpredictability, opportunities, and challenges. Recognizing the dynamic nature of life is the foundation of adaptive planning. Habits, while providing stability, must coexist harmoniously with the ever-shifting rhythm of personal and external circumstances.

External Factors Impacting Habits

External factors, such as career changes, family dynamics, and societal shifts, can exert profound influence on daily routines. A promotion at work may alter the structure of a typical day, and family commitments may fluctuate based on evolving priorities. The ability to adapt habits to accommodate external changes is essential for sustained progress.

For instance, someone aiming to establish a morning workout routine may face external challenges when work commitments necessitate early meetings. Adaptive planning allows for the seamless integration of workouts later in the day, preserving the commitment to fitness.

Internal Transitions and Growth

Internally, personal growth and transitions contribute to the dynamic nature of life. As individuals evolve, so do their values, aspirations, and priorities. A habit that once aligned perfectly with personal goals may require adaptation as individuals grow and embark on new phases of their journey.

Consider a person who cultivated a habit of daily journaling during a period of self-reflection and exploration. As they transition into a phase of increased professional responsibilities, adaptive planning may involve adjusting the format or frequency of journaling to align with the shifting focus of their life.

The Essence of Adaptive Planning

Adaptive planning transcends the rigidity of traditional planning methods. It embraces the philosophy that plans are not immutable laws, but flexible frameworks designed to accommodate change. The essence of adaptive planning lies in its responsiveness to evolving circumstances, fostering a symbiotic relationship between habits and the fluidity of life.

Flexibility vs. Rigidity in Planning

Rigid plans, while providing structure, can become barriers when confronted with change. Adaptive planning introduces flexibility, allowing individuals to pivot, adjust, and reimagine their strategies in response to shifting landscapes.

For instance, someone following a strict daily schedule may find it challenging to maintain their habits during a period of unexpected travel. An adaptive plan, however, allows for the modification of routines to suit the new environment and circumstances.

Iterative Nature of Adaptive Planning

Adaptive planning is iterative—a continuous process of refinement and adjustment. It involves periodic reviews, reflections, and recalibrations to ensure that plans remain aligned with current goals and circumstances. This iterative approach transforms planning into a dynamic and evolving companion on the habit change journey.

As an illustration, an individual committed to a reading habit may initially allocate a set time each evening for this activity. However, as life unfolds, an iterative approach involves revisiting the plan, recognizing changes in schedule, and adjusting reading sessions to more suitable times.

Strategies for Adaptive Planning in Habit Formation

Mastering the art of adaptive planning requires the integration of specific strategies into one's approach to habit formation. These strategies empower individuals to navigate change, overcome obstacles, and sustain their commitment to positive habits.

1. Goal Alignment Assessment: Regularly assess the alignment of habits with overarching goals. As priorities evolve, ensure that habits remain congruent with the current vision for personal development.

2. Periodic Habit Reviews: Conduct periodic reviews of established habits. Reflect on their impact, relevance, and consistency in light of changing circumstances. Adjust or redefine habits as needed to align with evolving aspirations.

3. Scenario Planning: Anticipate potential scenarios that may disrupt established routines. Develop contingency plans and alternative strategies to navigate challenges, ensuring that habits remain resilient in the face of unexpected events.

4. Adaptable Scheduling: Embrace adaptable scheduling that accommodates variability. Rather than adhering strictly to fixed timelines, allocate flexible time blocks for habit execution, allowing for adjustments based on daily fluctuations.

5. Mindful Response to Change: Cultivate a mindful response to change by approaching it with curiosity and adaptability. Instead of viewing change as an obstacle, perceive it as an opportunity to refine habits and explore new possibilities.

6. Feedback Integration: Incorporate feedback loops into habit formation. Actively seek feedback from personal reflections or external sources, using insights to refine habits and adapt plans for greater effectiveness.

7. Resource Optimization: Assess available resources, such as time, energy, and support systems. Optimize resource allocation to ensure that habits remain feasible and sustainable amid changing circumstances.

8. Continuous Learning Orientation: Embrace a continuous learning orientation. Treat setbacks and adaptations as opportunities for growth and refinement. Apply lessons learned to enhance the adaptability of future plans.

9. Holistic Life Integration: Integrate habits into the broader context of life. Rather than isolating habits, weave them seamlessly into daily routines, considering the interconnectedness of various aspects of life.

10. Community Engagement: Connect with a community or support network. Share experiences, challenges, and adaptive strategies with others pursuing similar habits. Collective wisdom enhances adaptability and resilience.

Real-Life Stories of Adaptive Planning

To illustrate the transformative power of adaptive planning, let's explore real-life stories of individuals who embraced change, adapted their plans, and continued their journey of habit formation.

Emily's Career Transition and Fitness Adaptation

Emily, navigating a significant career transition, faced challenges in maintaining her fitness habits. Recognizing the need for adaptive planning, she reassessed her goals and available time. Instead of adhering to a fixed workout schedule, Emily embraced adaptable scheduling.

She integrated shorter but more intense workouts during busy days and allocated longer sessions on days with more flexibility. This adaptive approach not only allowed Emily to navigate the demands of her career transition but also reinforced her commitment to fitness.

James' Evolving Writing Routine

James, an aspiring writer, experienced shifts in his writing routine as family responsibilities increased. Rather than viewing the changes as obstacles, James engaged in a goal alignment assessment. He realized the importance of adapting his writing habits to align with his current life phase.

James transitioned from long writing sessions to shorter, focused intervals. He integrated writing into moments of quietude during the day, demonstrating the power of adaptable scheduling and holistic life integration. This shift not only sustained James' writing practice but deepened its integration into his evolving life.

The Adaptive Planner's Journey

As Chapter 7 concludes, it becomes evident that adaptive planning is not a one-time endeavor but an ongoing journey. The adaptive planner recognizes that change is not a disruption but an inherent aspect of growth. By cultivating a mindset of adaptability, integrating flexible strategies, and embracing the iterative nature of planning, individuals embark on a transformative journey where habits evolve in tandem with the fluidity of life. In the realm of habit formation, adaptive planning emerges as the compass that guides individuals through the ever-changing landscapes of their personal development.

CHAPTER EIGHT

Chapter 8: The Ripple Effect of Keystone Habits: Transforming Lives One Habit at a Time

In the intricate tapestry of habit formation, certain habits wield extraordinary influence, transcending their individual impact to shape the entirety of one's life. Chapter 8 explores the concept of keystone habits—the powerful catalysts that trigger a ripple effect, instigating positive changes across various facets of existence. As we delve into the profound connections between habits and the transformative journey, readers will discover how identifying and nurturing keystone habits can become a cornerstone of lasting personal growth.

Unveiling the Concept of Keystone Habits

Keystone habits, a term popularized by Charles Duhigg in his book "The Power of Habit," refer to specific behaviors that, when adopted, have the potential to spark a cascade of positive changes. Unlike isolated habits, keystone habits serve as pivotal points, influencing other behaviors and aspects of life.

Characteristics of Keystone Habits

High Impact: Keystone habits have a disproportionately significant impact on overall well-being. They trigger positive changes that extend beyond the realm of specific behavior.

Domino Effect: Adopting a keystone habit initiates a domino effect, influencing other habits and creating a ripple of positive transformations in various areas of life.

Catalytic Influence: Keystone habits act as catalysts for broader lifestyle changes. They often serve as the foundation for building a framework of positive behaviors.

Identifying Keystone Habits

Identifying keystone habits involves recognizing behaviors that, when consistently practiced, lead to positive outcomes across multiple dimensions of life. While the specific keystone habits can vary from person to person, certain categories encompass common examples:

1. Physical Well-being:

Exercise Routine: Regular physical activity not only contributes to physical health but often leads to improved mood, increased energy, and enhanced cognitive function.

Nutrition Choices: Making conscious and healthy food choices can trigger a positive chain reaction, impacting energy levels, mental clarity, and overall well-being.

2. Mental and Emotional Health:

Mindfulness and Meditation: Practices that cultivate mindfulness and meditation can have a profound impact on stress reduction, emotional resilience, and mental clarity.

Journaling: Reflective journaling serves as a keystone habit, fostering self-awareness, emotional processing, and personal growth.

3. Productivity and Time Management:

Daily Planning: Planning and organizing daily tasks contribute to effective time management, reducing stress and enhancing productivity.

Prioritization: Prioritizing tasks and focusing on high-impact activities can lead to increased efficiency and goal achievement.

4. Relationship Building:

Expressing Gratitude: Regularly expressing gratitude fosters positive relationships, enhances well-being, and creates a supportive social environment.

Active Listening: Cultivating the habit of active listening strengthens communication skills and deepens interpersonal connections.

The Ripple Effect of Keystone Habits

1. Physical Transformation: The Exercise Ripple:

Adopting a regular exercise routine often triggers a cascade of positive changes. Physical activity not only improves cardiovascular health and muscle strength but also contributes to enhanced mood, better sleep, and increased energy levels. As individuals experience the physical benefits of exercise, they often find themselves naturally gravitating towards healthier food choices. The discipline and consistency cultivated through the exercise habit extends into other areas of life, fostering a holistic approach to well-being.

2. Mental Clarity and Emotional Resilience: The Mindfulness Ripple:

The practice of mindfulness and meditation serves as a keystone habit with far-reaching effects. As individuals incorporate mindfulness into their daily routine, they experience heightened self-awareness and emotional regulation. This newfound clarity often leads to improved decision-making, reduced stress levels, and a more positive outlook on life. The ripple effect extends to relationships, as individuals become more present and attuned to the needs of others, fostering deeper connections.

3. Time Mastery and Goal Achievement: The Planning Ripple:

Cultivating effective time management through daily planning sets in motion a ripple effect that transforms productivity and goal attainment. As individuals plan their days, they develop a sense of purpose and direction. This clarity in turn enhances focus and efficiency, leading to the accomplishment of tasks and goals. The ripple effect extends to increased self-confidence and a proactive mindset, reinforcing the belief that intentional planning is a key driver of success.

4. Strengthening Connections: The Gratitude Ripple:

The habit of expressing gratitude serves as a keystone behavior that ripples through the fabric of relationships. Regular expressions of gratitude create a positive and appreciative atmosphere, strengthening social bonds. As individuals acknowledge and appreciate the contributions of others, they contribute to a culture of positivity and support. The ripple effect extends to enhanced communication, increased collaboration, and the creation of a nurturing community.

Nurturing Keystone Habits for Lasting Transformation

Identifying keystone habits is the first step, but nurturing and sustaining them is equally crucial for lasting transformation. The following strategies provide a roadmap for cultivating and reinforcing keystone habits:

1. Start Small and Build Gradually:

Begin by incorporating small, manageable changes into your routine. Gradually build on these changes to establish the foundation for keystone habits. Starting small enhances the likelihood of long-term adherence.

2. Anchor Keystone Habits to Existing Routines:

Integrate keystone habits into existing daily routines. Anchoring new behaviors to established habits makes them more sustainable and reduces resistance to change.

3. Set Clear Intentions and Goals:

Clearly define the intentions and goals associated with each keystone habit. Having a compelling "why" enhances motivation and provides a roadmap for the transformative journey.

4. Establish Consistent Triggers:

Identify consistent triggers that prompt the initiation of keystone habits. Whether it's a specific time of day, a visual cue, or an existing routine, triggers create a reliable signal to engage in the desired behavior.

5. Monitor Progress and Celebrate Milestones:

Regularly monitor your progress in cultivating keystone habits. Celebrate milestones and acknowledge the positive changes experienced as a result of these habits. Positive reinforcement enhances motivation and commitment.

6. Adapt to Changing Circumstances:

Recognize that life is dynamic, and circumstances may change. Adapt keystone habits to align with evolving goals and priorities. Flexibility ensures that these habits remain relevant and impactful.

7. Share and Connect with Others:

Share your journey of cultivating keystone habits with others. Connect with a supportive community or accountability partner. Sharing experiences fosters a sense of camaraderie and provides additional motivation.

8. Practice Mindful Reflection:

Engage in mindful reflection on the impact of keystone habits on various aspects of your life. Regular reflection enhances self-awareness and reinforces the positive changes brought about by these influential behaviors.

9. Embrace Iterative Improvement:

View the process of nurturing keystone habits as an ongoing journey of iterative improvement. Continuously seek opportunities to refine and enhance these habits based on insights gained from your experiences.

10. Celebrate the Holistic Transformation:

Recognize that keystone habits are not isolated behaviors but catalysts for holistic transformation. Celebrate the interconnected positive changes in physical health

Conclusion: Keystone Habits - Transformative Melodies

Keystone habits compose the transformative melodies in the symphony of personal growth. Explored in Chapter 8, these influential behaviors, marked by high impact and a domino effect, orchestrate positive changes across life's dimensions.

From exercise sparking physical transformations to mindfulness fostering mental clarity, keystone habits act as catalysts for holistic change. Real-life stories like Sophia's and Alex's illustrate the profound impact, showcasing how these habits create ripples in health, relationships, and productivity.

Recognizing and cultivating keystone habits are essential in the journey of habit formation. The outlined strategies provide a roadmap for readers to compose their own symphony of personal growth.

In the next chapter, we explore the neuroscience behind habit formation, unraveling the intricate mechanisms that engrave habits into our daily lives. As you navigate this journey, may the symphony of keystone habits guide you towards a transformative crescendo of positive change

CHAPTER NINE

Chapter 9: Decoding Habits: The Neuroscientific Dance of Behavior

In the intricate dance of human behavior, habits play a starring role, driven by the complex interplay of neurons and brain circuits. Chapter 9 delves into the fascinating world of habit formation, decoding the neuroscientific mechanisms that underlie our daily routines. From the inception of a cue to the rhythmic dance of habit loops, this chapter unravels the neuroscience behind habits, offering insights into how behaviors become ingrained in the very fabric of our brains.

The Brain's Role in Habit Formation

Neurons and Synapses: The Choreographers of Behavior

At the heart of habit formation are neurons, the brain's communication specialists. Neurons communicate through synapses, creating a choreography of signals that shape our thoughts, emotions, and actions. As we engage in behaviors repeatedly, the dance of neurons and synapses orchestrates the transformation of actions into habits.

The Habit Loop: A Choreographed Sequence

The habit loop, a fundamental concept in habit formation, comprises three stages: cue, routine, and reward. Understanding this choreographed sequence provides a glimpse into the neural mechanisms of driving habits.

Cue: The initiation of a habit loop begins with a cue—a trigger that signals the brain to initiate a particular behavior. Cues can be external stimuli, internal emotions, or specific contexts that act as the starting point for habitual actions.

Routine: The routine is the behavior itself, the action prompted by the cue. As individuals repeat the routine in response to the cue, neural pathways are reinforced, creating a well-trodden path in the brain.

Reward: The reward serves as the reinforcement mechanism, providing a positive outcome that reinforces the habit loop. This pleasurable consequence strengthens the neural connections associated with the habit, making it more likely to be repeated in similar contexts.

Neural Plasticity: The Dance Floor of Habit Formation

The Malleability of Neural Networks

Neural plasticity, often referred to as the brain's ability to reorganize itself, is the dance floor where habits take shape. As behaviors are repeated, neural connections strengthen, creating efficient pathways for the habit loop. Understanding neural plasticity illuminates how the brain adapts to the demands of habit formation.

Habit Formation in the Basal Ganglia

The basal ganglia, a set of structures deep within the brain, plays a pivotal role in habit formation. This region is responsible for procedural memory, learning sequences of actions, and facilitating the automaticity of behaviors. As habits become ingrained, the basal ganglia take center stage, overseeing the execution of routines without conscious thought.

The Role of Dopamine: Habit's Dance Partner

Dopamine's Influence on Rewards

Dopamine, often hailed as the brain's pleasure chemical, is a key player in habit formation. The anticipation and experience of rewards trigger dopamine release, reinforcing the habit loop. The surge of pleasure associated with the reward creates a powerful incentive for the brain to seek out and repeat the associated behavior.

Dopamine's Dual Role: Motivation and Habit Reinforcement

Dopamine serves a dual role in the dance of habit formation. Beyond its role in immediate pleasure, dopamine acts as a motivational force, driving individuals to seek rewards and engage in habitual behaviors. The interplay between dopamine, rewards, and neural pathways solidifies habits, making them more resistant to change.

Breaking Down Habit Formation: Step by Step

Step 1: Cue Recognition

The first step in understanding and modifying habits involves recognizing the cues that trigger habitual behaviors. Cues can be categorized into:

Time: Habits triggered by specific times of the day.

Location: Habits associated with particular places or environments.

Emotional States: Behaviors linked to specific emotional states.

Other Habits: Existing habits serving as cues for subsequent behaviors.

Step 2: Routine Analysis

Once cues are identified, analyzing the routine—the habitual behavior itself—provides insights into the neural pathways involved. Questions to consider include:

What specific actions constitute the routine?

How automatic or conscious is the behavior?

What are the triggers within the routine that lead to the reward?

Step 3: Reward Evaluation

Understanding the reward associated with a habit is crucial. Rewards can be intrinsic (e.g., the pleasure of the behavior itself) or extrinsic (e.g., a tangible outcome). Evaluating the reward helps uncover the driving force behind the habit loop.

Step 4: Rewiring Neural Pathways

Armed with insights into cues, routines, and rewards, individuals can embark on rewiring neural pathways. Strategies for rewiring include:

Cue Manipulation: Modifying or replacing cues to disrupt the habitual sequence.

Routine Adjustment: Introducing alternative behaviors to replace or modify existing routines.

Reward Substitution: Finding alternative rewards that fulfill the same underlying need.

The Dance of Habit Change: Strategies for Success

Strategy 1: Gradual Progression

Attempting to overhaul habits overnight can be overwhelming. Gradual progression allows for sustainable change by focusing on small, manageable adjustments over time. This approach aligns with the brain's capacity for adaptation and minimizes resistance to change.

Strategy 2: Consistent Repetition

Neural pathways strengthen through consistent repetition. Repetition is the rehearsal that engrains new habits into the brain's dance routine. Regular practice reinforces the rewiring of neural connections, making the new behavior more automatic over time.

Strategy 3: Positive Reinforcement

Positive reinforcement leverages the brain's reward system to encourage habit change. Celebrating small victories and acknowledging progress activates the brain's pleasure centers, reinforcing the rewiring of neural pathways associated with the desired behavior.

Strategy 4: Accountability and Support

Engaging in habit change alongside others provides accountability and support. Social connections influence behavior through shared cues, routines, and rewards. Having a supportive community enhances motivation and fosters a collaborative dance of habit change.

Strategy 5: Mindfulness Practices

Incorporating mindfulness practices enhances awareness of habits and their underlying cues, routines, and rewards. Mindfulness cultivates a non-judgmental observation of behaviors, creating space for intentional choices and increased self-awareness.

Strategy 6: Adaptive Planning

Recognizing the dynamic nature of habit formation, adaptive planning anticipates potential challenges and adjusts strategies accordingly. Flexibility in approach acknowledges that setbacks are part of the dance and allows for resilient adaptation.

Real-Life Stories of Habit Transformation

To illuminate the neuroscience of habit change, let's explore real-life stories of individuals who successfully rewired their habits.

Sarah's Caffeine Habit: Rewiring the Morning Routine

Sarah, recognizing her reliance on caffeine as a morning ritual, decided to rewire this habit. Identifying the cue (waking up), routine (making coffee), and reward (energy boost), she introduced a new routine—morning stretches and hydration. Gradually, Sarah's brain adapted to the new sequence, associating waking up with a refreshing stretch rather than the immediate need for caffeine.

Robert's Smartphone Addiction: Rewiring Cue and Routine

Robert, grappling with smartphone addiction triggered by boredom (cue), analyzed his routine of mindless scrolling and constant notifications. Rewiring the cue involved introducing more engaging activities during downtime. He replaced the routine of excessive phone use with reading a book or practicing a hobby. Over time, the brain adapted to the new routine, reducing the automatic response to smartphone usage.

Conclusion: A Symphony of Adaptation

As Chapter 9 concludes, the intricate dance of habit formation emerges as a symphony of neural adaptation. From the initiation of cues to the rhythmic routine and the harmonious reward, habits are choreographed by the brain's plasticity and the influence of dopamine.

Understanding the neuroscience behind habits provides a roadmap for intentional rewiring. By recognizing cues, analyzing routines, evaluating rewards, and implementing strategic change, individuals can take the lead in the dance of habit transformation. The strategies outlined, coupled with real-life stories, illuminate the potential for rewiring neural pathways and orchestrating a symphony of adaptation.

In the upcoming chapter, we explore the influence of environment and external factors on habit formation. By understanding how our surroundings shape behaviors, we gain deeper insights into the dance between internal neural processes and external influences in the grand choreography of habits

CHAPTER TEN

Chapter 10: The Dance of Environment: Shaping Habits in the Theater of Life

In the intricate theater of habit formation, the stage is not limited to the neural dance within our brains. Chapter 10 explores the profound influence of our external environment on the choreography of habits. From the design of our living spaces to the cultural rhythms of society, this chapter delves into how the external stage sets the scene for the dance of behaviors, affecting the initiation, routine, and reinforcement of habits.

The Environmental Stage

Home and Workspaces: Habit Arenas

Our immediate surroundings, whether at home or work, serve as the primary arenas where habits unfold. The design, layout, and accessibility of these spaces influence the cues that trigger habits. Understanding the role of environmental cues is essential for shaping behaviors within these habitual arenas.

Cues in Home Spaces: The arrangement of items, the visibility of healthy snacks, and the presence of exercise equipment all act as cues that influence habits.

Cues in Workspaces: The organization of desks, the availability of healthy food options, and the presence of visual prompts impact habits in professional environments.

Cultural and Social Landscapes: Collective Habitual Rhythms

Beyond individual spaces, the broader cultural and social landscapes contribute to the collective dance of habits. Cultural norms, societal expectations, and shared rituals shape the behaviors of communities and influence the formation of habits on a larger scale.

Cultural Eating Habits: The types of food considered customary in a culture can significantly impact individual dietary habits.

Societal Fitness Norms: The prevalence of fitness-related activities within a society can influence individual exercise habits.

Community Well-being Practices: Shared habits within communities, such as volunteering or communal events, contribute to the overall well-being of the population.

The Power of Environmental Cues

Cue Visibility and Accessibility

The visibility and accessibility of cues play a crucial role in habit initiation. Environmental cues act as signals that prompt the brain to initiate specific behaviors. Understanding how cues are presented in our surroundings can guide intentional changes in habit formation.

Visible Cues: Items placed prominently, such as a bowl of fruit on the kitchen counter, serve as visual cues for healthy eating.

Accessible Cues: Making desired behaviors more accessible, such as placing running shoes by the door, increases the likelihood of habit initiation.

Habit Stacking: Leveraging Existing Cues

Habit stacking involves linking a new behavior to an existing habit or cue, capitalizing on established routines. This strategy utilizes the power of environmental cues to prompt the initiation of desired habits.

Example: Attaching a new habit of stretching to the existing routine of brewing morning coffee.

Designing Habit-Friendly Environments

The Psychology of Color and Design

The aesthetics and design of our environments can influence our emotional states and, consequently, our habits. The psychology of color and spatial arrangement plays a role in shaping the emotional context within which habits unfold.

Color Impact: Warm colors may evoke energy and motivation, while cool colors can promote relaxation and focus.

Spatial Arrangement: An organized and clutter-free space can contribute to a sense of calm and order, positively impacting habit formation.

Nudging and Choice Architecture

Nudging involves subtle changes in the environment to encourage specific behaviors without restricting choice. Choice architecture focuses on the intentional design of environments to promote healthier decisions.

Nudging Examples: Placing healthy snacks at eye level in a pantry or using smaller plates to encourage portion control.

Choice Architecture Examples: Designing workplace cafeterias to highlight nutritious options and making stairs more accessible than elevators.

Social Influences on Habit Formation

Social Norms and Peer Influence

The behaviors of those around us, whether family, friends, or colleagues, can significantly impact our habits. Social norms and peer influence create a shared environment that either supports or challenges individual habit formation.

Family Dynamics: Family habits, such as mealtime routines or recreational activities, contribute to the formation of individual habits.

Workplace Culture: The collective habits within a workplace influence individual behaviors, including break time activities and stress management practices.

Accountability Partners and Support Networks

Engaging in habit change with accountability partners or within a support network enhances the environmental influence on behaviors. Shared goals and collaborative efforts create a positive ecosystem for habit formation.

Accountability Partners: Individuals working together to achieve similar habits can provide mutual support and encouragement.

Support Networks: Community-based programs, online forums, or social groups centered around specific habits offer a sense of belonging and shared commitment.

Creating a Habit-Optimized Lifestyle

Rituals and Routines: Structuring Daily Life

Intentionally structuring daily rituals and routines contributes to an environment conducive to habit formation. Consistent patterns of behavior create a framework within which habits can take root and flourish.

Morning Rituals: Establishing a set routine in the morning can set a positive tone for the day and facilitate habit initiation.

Evening Rituals: Wind-down routines in the evening create a conducive environment for habits like relaxation or sleep hygiene.

Environmental Detox: Removing Habitual Barriers

Identifying and eliminating environmental barriers to desired habits is essential for successful habit formation. An environmental detox involves streamlining surroundings to reduce obstacles and enhance the ease of habit initiation.

Decluttering Spaces: A clutter-free environment minimizes distractions and supports focused engagement in habit-related activities.

Digital Environment Audit: Evaluating digital spaces to reduce distractions and enhance focus on desired habits.

Real-Life Stories of Environmental Habit Transformation

To illustrate the impact of environmental cues on habit formation, let's explore real-life stories of individuals who transformed their habits by intentionally shaping their surroundings.

Maya's Home Gym Transformation

Maya, aiming to establish a consistent exercise habit, transformed a spare room into a home gym. By making exercise equipment visible and easily accessible, Maya created a cue that prompted regular workouts. The intentional design of her home environment played a crucial role in solidifying the exercise habit.

Carlos' Workplace Healthy Eating Initiative

Carlos, concerned about unhealthy eating habits at work, initiated a workplace wellness campaign. By collaborating with colleagues and implementing choice architecture in the office cafeteria, Carlos positively influenced the eating habits of his team. The redesigned environment nudged individuals towards healthier food choices, contributing to a collective shift in workplace eating habits.

Conclusion: Orchestrating Habitual Harmony in Environments

As Chapter 10 takes its final bow, the role of external environments in shaping the dance of habits becomes evident. From the cues embedded in our living spaces to the cultural rhythms that surround us, environments act as influential choreographers in the theater of life.

Understanding the power of environmental cues allows individuals to intentionally design spaces that support desired habits. Whether through habit stacking, choice architecture, or environmental detox, the shaping of environments becomes a strategic dance that enhances the ease and success of habit formation.

In the subsequent chapter, we explore the concept of habit sustainability—how habits can endure over time and become integral components of a fulfilling and purposeful life. As the dance of habits continues, may the intentional design of environments contribute to the harmonious orchestration of behaviors in the grand theater of life

CHAPTER ELEVEN

Chapter 11: Sustaining the Dance: The Art and Science of Habit Longevity

In the intricate choreography of habit formation, the true measure of success lies in sustainability. Chapter 11 delves into the art and science of habit longevity, exploring the factors that contribute to the endurance of behaviors over time. From the psychology of habit adherence to the role of intrinsic motivation, this chapter unravels the secrets to sustaining the dance of habits for the long haul.

The Psychology of Habit Adherence

The Habit Identity: Aligning with Self-Perception

The integration of a habit into one's identity is a powerful driver of long-term adherence. When a behavior aligns with an individual's self-perception, the habit becomes an intrinsic part of who they are, fostering a sense of consistency and authenticity.

Example: Someone who perceives themselves as an active and health-conscious individual is more likely to adhere to an exercise habit that aligns with this identity.

Consistency as a Mental Anchor

Consistency creates a mental anchor for habits. When behaviors become routine and predictable, the brain perceives them as integral parts of daily life. This mental anchoring enhances the likelihood of habit sustainability.

Routine Integration: Embedding habits within existing routines contributes to their consistency and integration into daily life.

Intrinsic vs. Extrinsic Motivation

Intrinsic Motivation: The Heartbeat of Habit Sustainability

Intrinsic motivation, driven by internal rewards such as personal satisfaction and a sense of accomplishment, is a potent force for sustaining habits. When individuals derive joy or fulfillment from the habit itself, they are more likely to persist in the long term.

Example: Someone practicing a creative hobby for the sheer joy of expression is intrinsically motivated.

Extrinsic Motivation: The Role of External Rewards

While extrinsic rewards, such as recognition or tangible outcomes, can initially boost motivation, long-term habit sustainability often relies on a balance between intrinsic and extrinsic factors.

Example: Receiving praise for a fitness achievement can serve as an extrinsic motivator initially, but the habit endures when the individual discovers intrinsic enjoyment in the activity.

The Role of Feedback Mechanisms

Real-Time Feedback: Course Correction in the Dance

Immediate feedback during habit performance provides individuals with valuable information for course correction. Whether positive or constructive, real-time feedback enhances awareness and refines the habit execution.

Examples of Real-Time Feedback: Tracking progress through a habit-tracking app or receiving immediate responses in a learning context.

Reflective Feedback: Cultivating Self-Awareness

Periodic reflection on habit progress contributes to self-awareness and a deeper understanding of the habit's impact. Engaging in mindful assessment fosters adaptability and a commitment to continuous improvement.

Reflective Questions: What benefits have been experienced? What challenges were faced, and how were they addressed?

The Role of Rituals in Habit Sustainability

Rituals as Habit Anchors

Incorporating rituals into habit structures creates anchors that signal the beginning or conclusion of a behavior. Rituals provide a sense of ceremony and contribute to the habit's perceived significance.

Example: A brief meditation ritual before starting a work task serves as an anchor for a focus-oriented habit.

Celebratory Rituals: Acknowledging Milestones

Acknowledging and celebrating milestones, both small and significant, reinforces the positive aspects of habit adherence. Celebratory rituals contribute to a positive feedback loop, strengthening the emotional connection to the habit.

Celebratory Rituals: Sharing achievements with a supportive community, treating oneself to a small reward, or engaging in a special activity.

Addressing Challenges: The Dance of Resilience

Anticipating Setbacks: A Normal Part of the Dance

Understanding that setbacks are a natural part of habit formation helps individuals approach challenges with resilience. Anticipating potential obstacles allows for proactive strategies and minimizes the impact of setbacks on long-term adherence.

Resilience Strategies: Having contingency plans, seeking support during challenging times, and reframing setbacks as learning opportunities.

Adaptive Adjustments: Tweaking the Dance Steps

The ability to adapt and adjust strategies based on evolving circumstances is crucial for sustaining habits. Recognizing the dynamic nature of life allows individuals to modify habits to align with changing priorities and environments.

Adaptive Strategies: Modifying the frequency or intensity of a habit, adjusting the habit's time or location, or exploring alternative routines.

Social Dynamics and Habit Sustainability

Community Support: The Dance of Collective Adherence

Engaging in habit formation within a supportive community or social network enhances sustainability. Shared experiences, encouragement, and accountability contribute to the collective adherence of habits.

Community Platforms: Online forums, group challenges, or local clubs centered around specific habits foster a sense of shared commitment.

Social Modeling: Learning from the Dance of Others

Observing and learning from the habits of others can provide inspiration and insights. Social modeling contributes to the normalization of desired behaviors and reinforces their sustainability.

Role Models: Identifying individuals who exhibit long-term adherence to similar habits can serve as motivational role models.

The Intersection of Mindfulness and Habit Sustainability

Present Moment Awareness: The Essence of Mindful Habits

Mindfulness, or present moment awareness, enhances habit sustainability by cultivating a deep connection to the present experience. Being fully engaged in the habit performance reduces distraction and increases the habit's intrinsic value.

Mindful Practices: Incorporating mindful breathing, focused attention, or sensory awareness into habit execution.

Intentional Choices: The Mindful Selection of Habits

Mindful habit selection involves intentionally choosing behaviors that align with one's values and long-term well-being. This deliberate approach contributes to sustained commitment and fulfillment.

Reflection Questions: How does this habit align with my values? What long-term impact does it have on my well-being?

Real-Life Stories of Habit Longevity

To illustrate the principles of habit sustainability, let's explore real-life stories of individuals who have successfully maintained habits over the long term.

Elena's Daily Writing Ritual

Elena, an aspiring writer, established a daily writing habit as part of her morning routine. By incorporating a simple and enjoyable writing ritual, such as enjoying a cup of tea and playing soft music, Elena made the habit a cherished and intrinsic part of her identity. The consistency of her ritual and the intrinsic joy derived from creative expression have sustained Elena's writing habit for years.

Mark's Fitness Journey: Balancing Intrinsic and Extrinsic Motivation

Mark, initially motivated by extrinsic factors like weight loss, transitioned to a more sustainable fitness journey by discovering the intrinsic joy of movement. Incorporating activities, he genuinely enjoyed, such as dancing and hiking, Mark found lasting motivation that went beyond external outcomes. The balance between intrinsic and extrinsic motivation has contributed to the enduring nature of Mark's active lifestyle.

Conclusion: The Timeless Dance of Habit

As Chapter 11 takes its final bow, the essence of sustaining the dance of habits emerges as a delicate interplay between psychology, motivation, and environmental influences. From the alignment with identity to the balance of intrinsic and extrinsic motivation, the journey of habit longevity involves a nuanced and intentional choreography.

Understanding the psychology of habit adherence, leveraging feedback mechanisms, incorporating rituals, addressing challenges with resilience, and embracing social dynamics contribute to the sustainability of habits over time. The intersection of mindfulness and habit sustainability adds a layer of depth, emphasizing the importance of present moment awareness and intentional choices in the dance of enduring behaviors.

In the forthcoming chapter, we explore the concept of habit evolution—how habits adapt and transform over the course of a lifetime. As the dance of habits continues, may the principles of sustainability guide you in crafting a timeless and fulfilling repertoire of behaviors.

CHAPTER TWELVE

Chapter 12: Evolutionary Rhythms: The Lifelong Dance of Habit Transformation

In the grand tapestry of human experience, habits are not static entities but dynamic, ever-evolving patterns that weave through the various stages of life. Chapter 12 explores the concept of habit evolution, delving into how behaviors adapt and transform over the course of a lifetime. From the influence of life transitions to the role of personal growth, this chapter uncovers the nuances of the lifelong dance of habit transformation.

The Impact of Life Transitions

The Ebb and Flow of Change

Life transitions, whether marked by milestones, career shifts, relationships, or health changes, introduce new rhythms to the dance of habits. Understanding the impact of these transitions is crucial for navigating the evolving landscape of behaviors.

Examples of Life Transitions: Marriage, parenthood, retirement, relocation, or significant health events.

Adaptation Strategies: Navigating Transitory Phases

Adapting habits to align with the demands of life transitions involves intentional strategies. Flexibility, self-compassion, and a willingness to reevaluate existing habits contribute to a smoother adjustment during periods of change.

Adaptation Strategies: Gradual adjustments, setting realistic expectations, and seeking support during transitional phases.

The Role of Personal Growth in Habit Evolution

Continuous Learning: The Catalyst for Change

A commitment to lifelong learning and personal growth serves as a catalyst for habit evolution. Embracing new skills, knowledge, and perspectives introduces fresh dimensions to the dance, prompting the reevaluation and transformation of existing habits.

Learning Platforms: Formal education, online courses, workshops, and mentorship programs.

Goal Setting and Habit Alignment

As individuals evolve personally and professionally, aligning habits with overarching goals becomes essential. Goal setting provides a roadmap for intentional habit evolution, ensuring that behaviors remain congruent with evolving aspirations.

SMART Goals: Specific, Measurable, Achievable, Relevant, Time-bound goals guide habit alignment.

The Interplay Between External and Internal Influences

External Influences: Shaping Habit Dynamics

External factors, including societal trends, technological advancements, and cultural shifts, influence the external context within which habits unfold. Understanding and adapting to these external influences contribute to the ongoing evolution of behaviors.

Examples of External Influences: Technological innovations, social media trends, and changes in workplace dynamics.

Internal Influences: The Inner Compass of Values

The evolving alignment of habits with personal values serves as an internal compass guiding habit evolution. As individuals gain clarity on their values, habits naturally transform to reflect these intrinsic guiding principles.

Values Exploration: Reflecting on core beliefs and priorities to inform habit choices.

The Dance of Flexibility and Resilience

Flexibility: The Art of Adaptive Choreography

Embracing flexibility in habit formation involves an openness to experimentation and adjustment. Flexible habits adapt to changing circumstances, fostering a sense of spontaneity and adaptability in dance.

Flexibility Practices: Trying new activities, exploring varied routines, and being open to habit experimentation.

Resilience: Bouncing Back from Setbacks

Resilience is a vital quality in the dance of habit evolution. Recognizing that setbacks are inevitable, building resilience allows individuals to bounce back from challenges and continue the forward momentum of habit transformation.

Resilience Building Strategies: Mindfulness practices, self-reflection, and learning from setbacks.

The Impact of Social and Cultural Dynamics

Social Networks: Co-Creators of Habit Narratives

Social dynamics, including peer influence, family habits, and community norms, play a pivotal role in habit evolution. Shared experiences within social networks contribute to collective habits that evolve over time.

Community Engagement: Participating in shared habits within communities or social circles.

Cultural Narratives: Influencing Habit Storylines

Cultural shifts and narratives shape the overarching storylines of habits within societies. As cultural perspectives on health, work, and lifestyle evolve, individual habits adapt to align with these broader narratives.

Cultural Considerations: Changing attitudes toward health, sustainability, and work-life balance.

The Influence of Technology on Habit Evolution

Tech-Driven Habits: Navigating Digital Landscapes

The integration of technology into daily life introduces new possibilities and challenges in habit formation. Understanding the impact of technology on behaviors and incorporating digital mindfulness contributes to the mindful evolution of tech-driven habits.

Examples of Tech-Driven Habits: Screen time management, digital fitness routines, and online learning.

Technological Innovations: Catalysts for Change

Technological innovations, from wearable devices to habit-tracking apps, serve as catalysts for habit evolution. Leveraging technology mindfully enhances self-awareness and provides tools for intentional behavior modification.

Mindful Tech Use: Setting digital boundaries, using habit-tracking apps, and incorporating tech-free moments.

The Wisdom of Aging and Habit Refinement

Aging Gracefully: The Dance of Wisdom

As individuals age, habits often undergo a natural refinement process. Priorities shift, and the focus may transition from ambitious goal pursuit to the cultivation of meaningful and fulfilling habits that contribute to overall well-being.

Wisdom Practices: Incorporating mindfulness, gratitude, and reflective habits into daily life.

Intergenerational Influences: Passing Down Habit Legacies

Intergenerational influences shape the dance of habits as individuals pass down learned behaviors and values to younger generations. Recognizing the impact of familial and cultural legacies contributes to conscious habit evolution.

Family Rituals: Passing down traditions, values, and habit practices within families.

Real-Life Stories of Habit Evolution

To illustrate the principles of habit evolution, let's explore real-life stories of individuals who have navigated transformative phases in their habits.

Sarah's Career Transition and Habit Pivot

Sarah, navigating a career transition, found herself reevaluating her work-related habits. Recognizing the need for skill development in a new field, she embraced the habit of continuous learning. This adaptive habit allowed Sarah to not only navigate the challenges of the career shift but also thrive in her evolving professional landscape.

James' Retirement Reflection and Lifestyle Evolution

Upon retirement, James underwent a reflective period, redefining his priorities and values. His habit of daily exercise transformed from a fitness goal-driven routine to a more mindful and enjoyable practice. James embraced nature walks, yoga, and leisurely bike rides, aligning his habits with a newfound sense of balance and well-being.

Conclusion: A Lifelong Symphony of Habit Transformation

As Chapter 12 takes its final bow, the concept of habit evolution emerges as a dynamic and lifelong symphony. From the impact of life transitions to the role of personal growth, the dance of habits weaves through the various stages of life, adapting and transforming with the rhythms of experience.

Understanding the interplay between external and internal influences, embracing flexibility and resilience, acknowledging the role of social and cultural dynamics, and navigating the impact of technology contribute to the intentional evolution of habits

The wisdom of aging and the passing down of habit legacies further enrich the narrative of the lifelong dance of habit transformation.

In the upcoming chapter, we explore the concept of habit legacy—how individuals can consciously shape and leave a positive impact through their habits. As the dance of habits continues, may the symphony of evolution guide you in crafting a rich and purposeful habit repertoire throughout the journey of life.

CHAPTER THIRTEEN

Chapter 13: Leaving a Positive Mark: The Power of Habit Legacy

In this chapter, we explore how the habits we cultivate can extend beyond our own lives, creating a positive impact for future generations. Let's delve into the simple yet profound aspects of habit legacy, understanding how everyday behaviors can shape a lasting mark on the world.

The Ripple Effect of Everyday Habits

Small Actions, Big Impact

Even the simplest habits can have a ripple effect, influencing not only our immediate surroundings but also the broader community. From smiling at strangers to acts of kindness, these everyday behaviors contribute to a positive habit legacy.

Example: Regularly picking up litter in a local park can inspire others to do the same, creating a cleaner and more pleasant environment for everyone.

Teaching by Doing

Our habits often serve as silent teachers, conveying values and behaviors to those around us. Whether at home, in the workplace, or within a community, the way we live our lives leaves an imprint on others, shaping their perspectives and actions.

Example: A parent who practices healthy eating habits instills a similar mindset in their children, fostering a generational legacy of well-being.

The Role of Intentionality in Habit Legacy

Purposeful Habits: A Legacy Blueprint

Being intentional about the habits we cultivate allows us to craft a deliberate legacy. Choosing behaviors that align with our values and contribute positively to the world ensures that our habit legacy reflects the impact we wish to leave behind.

Example: Consistently volunteering for community service projects establishes a legacy of selflessness and civic responsibility.

Shared Values, Shared Legacy

Aligning habits with shared values within a family, community, or organization strengthens the collective impact of a habit legacy. When individuals come together with a common purpose, the legacy becomes a shared narrative that extends far beyond individual actions.

Example: A group of coworkers who prioritize sustainability can collectively reduce their environmental footprint, leaving a shared legacy of ecological responsibility.

Creating Lasting Memories Through Habit

Rituals and Traditions: Timeless Legacies

Incorporating rituals and traditions into daily life creates lasting memories that contribute to a meaningful habit legacy. These shared experiences become touchstones for future generations, fostering a sense of continuity and connection.

Example: Family dinners, holiday traditions, or annual celebrations can form the foundation of a positive habit legacy.

Documenting Habits: A Living Legacy

Recording and sharing our habits, experiences, and life lessons through writing, videos, or other media preserves a tangible legacy. These documented insights provide guidance and inspiration for those who come after us.

Example: Keeping a journal about personal growth, challenges, and triumphs can serve as a valuable legacy for family members or the broader community.

The Generational Impact of Habit Legacy

Passing Down Wisdom Through Habits

As habits are passed down from one generation to the next, they become vessels of accumulated wisdom. Each generation builds upon the habits of the past, contributing to a legacy of shared knowledge and values.

Example: Learning a family recipe or engaging in a traditional craft can pass down cultural heritage and skills through generations.

Mentorship and Role Modeling

Acting as mentors and positive role models amplifies the impact of habit legacy. By guiding and inspiring others, individuals contribute not only to their immediate circle but also to the broader community, leaving a lasting imprint on the lives they touch.

Example: A mentor who instills the habit of continuous learning can influence the professional and personal growth of their mentees.

The Intersection of Individual and Collective Legacy

Harmony in Diversity

Individual habit legacies, when woven together, create a rich tapestry of collective impact. Embracing diversity in habits allows for a harmonious blending of individual stories, forming a legacy that resonates with the complexity of human experience.

Example: A community where individuals practice diverse habits related to cultural celebrations, artistic expressions, and community service creates a vibrant collective legacy.

Collaborative Legacy Building

Collaboration and shared endeavors enhance the potency of habit legacies. By working together toward common goals and values, individuals contribute to a collective legacy that transcends individual achievements.

Example: A group of friends who collectively engage in charitable activities establishes a collaborative habit legacy of compassion and community service.

The Enduring Spirit of Simple Habits

Simplicity and Longevity

Simple habits, rooted in kindness, gratitude, and empathy, have an enduring quality. These foundational behaviors, accessible to everyone, form the backbone of a habit legacy that stands the test of time.

Example: Expressing gratitude, lending a helping hand, or practicing active listening are simple yet impactful habits that contribute to a positive legacy.

A Lasting Invitation

As Chapter 13 comes to a close, the essence of habit legacy lies in the invitation it extends to future generations. Simple, intentional actions, whether individual or collective, create a ripple effect that shapes the world for years to come.

In the final chapter, we explore the concept of reflective habits—practices that foster introspection and mindfulness, adding depth to the journey of habit formation and legacy building. As the dance of habits continues, may the legacy you create be a testament to the positive mark you leave on the world.

CHAPTER FOURTEEN

Chapter 14: Reflective Habits: Nurturing Mindfulness and Self-Discovery

In this chapter, we explore the transformative power of reflective habits—simple practices that foster introspection, mindfulness, and self-discovery. These habits provide a pathway to deeper understanding, allowing individuals to navigate the complexities of life with clarity and purpose.

The Essence of Reflective Habits

Introspection as a Guiding Light

Reflective habits center around the art of introspection, turning one's attention inward to gain insight into thoughts, emotions, and experiences. These habits serve as a compass for personal growth and well-being.

Example: Taking a few minutes each day to journal thoughts and feelings fosters self-awareness and emotional clarity.

The Role of Mindfulness

Mindfulness, a key component of reflective habits, involves being fully present in the current moment. By cultivating a mindful approach to daily activities, individuals can enhance focus, reduce stress, and deepen their connection to their inner selves.

Example: Practicing mindful breathing during routine tasks, such as washing dishes, promotes a sense of calm and presence.

Building a Reflective Routine

Morning Reflection: Setting Intentions

Incorporating reflective habits into the morning routine sets a positive tone for the day. This intentional practice allows individuals to set clear intentions, aligning their actions with their values.

Example: Taking a few moments each morning to reflect on goals and express gratitude establishes a positive mindset for the day ahead.

Evening Reflection: Cultivating Gratitude

Evening reflection rituals provide an opportunity to review the day's events, express gratitude, and identify areas for growth. Cultivating gratitude enhances overall well-being and contributes to a positive mindset.

Example: Keeping a gratitude journal and reflecting on three things to be thankful for each night fosters a sense of appreciation.

The Art of Journaling

The Journal as a Reflective Canvas

Journaling is a powerful reflective habit that allows individuals to explore their thoughts, emotions, and experiences in a written format. The act of putting pen to paper can bring clarity and insights that may not surface through verbal expression alone.

Example: Keeping a daily journal to document thoughts, experiences, and goals provides a tangible record of personal growth.

Prompts for Reflection

Using reflective prompts in journaling or contemplative practices can guide individuals in exploring specific aspects of their lives. Thoughtful prompts encourage deeper self-reflection and help uncover meaningful insights.

Example Prompts: "What brought me joy today?" or "What challenges did I face, and how can I approach them differently in the future?"

Mindful Movement and Reflection

Integrating Reflection into Physical Activities

Reflective habits need not be confined to stillness; they can be seamlessly integrated into physical activities. Mindful movement, such as walking or yoga, becomes an opportunity for contemplation and self-discovery.

Example: Practicing mindful walking by paying attention to each step and breath, fostering a sense of presence during the activity.

Body Scan Meditation

Body scan meditation is a reflective practice that involves directing attention to different parts of the body, noticing sensations, and promoting relaxation. This mindfulness technique enhances self-awareness and reduces tension.

Example: Allocating time for a brief body scan meditation before bedtime can promote relaxation and improve sleep quality.

Reflection Through Creative Expression

Artistic Outlets for Self-Expression

Creative activities provide an avenue for reflective expression. Whether through visual arts, writing, or music, engaging in creative pursuits allows individuals to explore and communicate their inner thoughts and emotions.

Example: Creating a visual journal, incorporating drawings and images, becomes a unique form of reflective self-expression.

Music and Mindful Listening

Listening to music mindfully, with full attention and intention, can be a reflective habit that enhances emotional awareness. Exploring different genres or creating personalized playlists can evoke specific moods and reflections.

Example: Setting aside time to listen to a favorite piece of music and reflecting on the emotions it evokes.

Guided Reflection and Meditation

Utilizing Guided Practices

Guided reflection and meditation sessions provide structured support for individuals seeking a more directed approach to introspection. Various apps, podcasts, or recorded sessions offer guided practices to enhance mindfulness and self-awareness.

Example: Participating in a guided meditation session focused on self-compassion and acceptance.

Gratitude Meditation

Gratitude meditation involves intentionally reflecting on the things one is thankful for. This practice cultivates a positive mindset and encourages individuals to appreciate the abundance in their lives.

Example: Spending a few minutes each day meditating on specific aspects of life to be grateful for, fostering a sense of contentment.

Social Reflection and Connection

Reflecting on Relationships

Reflective habits extend to social interactions, prompting individuals to consider the quality of their relationships and the impact they have on others. Mindful communication and empathetic reflection enhance the dynamics of social connections.

Example: Reflecting on recent interactions and considering how to enhance positive communication in relationships.

Group Reflection Practices

Engaging in reflective practices within a group or community setting fosters collective growth. Group reflection allows for shared insights, support, and a sense of connection in the journey of self-discovery.

Example: Participating in a group discussion or workshop focused on reflective habits and personal growth.

Navigating Challenges Through Reflection

Reflection as a Tool for Resilience

Reflective habits contribute to resilience by providing a space for individuals to process challenges, learn from setbacks, and develop adaptive strategies. This introspective approach enables a constructive response to life's difficulties.

Example: Journaling about challenging experiences and identifying lessons learned to navigate similar situations in the future.

Seeking Professional Guidance

In certain situations, seeking the support of a therapist, counselor, or life coach can enhance the reflective process. Professional guidance provides individuals with tools and insights to navigate complex emotions and challenges.

Example: Engaging in reflective therapy sessions to explore deeper aspects of personal growth and well-being.

Real-Life Stories of Reflective Transformation

To illustrate the impact of reflective habits, let's explore real-life stories of individuals who have experienced transformative journeys through introspection and mindfulness.

Emily's Journaling Ritual for Emotional Well-Being

Struggling with anxiety and stress, Emily incorporated a daily journaling ritual into her routine. Through reflective writing, she identified patterns of thought that contributed to her anxiety and developed strategies to manage stress. Over time, this simple reflective habit became a cornerstone of Emily's emotional well-being.

Javier's Mindful Walking Practice for Clarity

Facing a challenging career decision, Javier turned to mindful walking as a reflective practice. Each day, he took a mindful walk-in nature, allowing the rhythmic movement to clear his mind. This practice not only brought clarity to his decision-making process but also became a source of daily serenity.

Conclusion: A Journey of Continuous Reflection

As Chapter 14 concludes, the essence of reflective habits lies in their ability to foster mindfulness, self-discovery, and resilience. Whether through journaling, mindfulness practices, creative expression, or social reflection, these habits provide a compass for navigating life with intention and awareness.

In the final chapter, we explore the concept of lifelong learning habits—practices that embrace curiosity, growth, and the pursuit of knowledge throughout the entirety of one's journey. As the dance of habits continues, may reflective practices illuminate your path, guiding you toward a deeper understanding of yourself and the world around you

CHAPTER FIFTEEN

Chapter 15: Lifelong Learning Habits: Nurturing Curiosity and Growth

Chapter 15: Lifelong Learning Habits: Nurturing Curiosity and Growth

In this concluding chapter, we explore the transformative power of lifelong learning habits—simple practices that embrace curiosity, foster personal growth, and encourage the pursuit of knowledge throughout every stage of life. These habits serve as a perpetual wellspring of inspiration, enriching the journey of continuous learning.

The Significance of Lifelong Learning

Curiosity as a Lifelong Companion

Lifelong learning begins with a fundamental trait: curiosity. Cultivating a curious mindset allows individuals to approach life with a sense of wonder, opening doors to new knowledge and experiences.

Example: Asking questions, exploring diverse topics, and maintaining a genuine interest in the world are manifestations of a curious mindset.

The Evolving Nature of Knowledge

In a rapidly changing world, the nature of knowledge is dynamic and ever evolving. Lifelong learners recognize the importance of staying informed, adapting to new information, and embracing the joy of discovery.

Example: Embracing technological advancements, exploring emerging fields, and staying informed about global issues contribute to a proactive approach to learning.

The Foundations of Lifelong Learning Habits

Embracing Curricular and Extracurricular Learning

Lifelong learning encompasses both formal and informal avenues of education. While formal education provides structured knowledge, extracurricular learning through hobbies, interests, and diverse experiences adds depth to one's understanding of the world.

Example: Balancing academic pursuits with hobbies such as reading, painting, or learning a musical instrument creates a well-rounded approach to lifelong learning.

Setting Personal Learning Goals

Establishing personal learning goals empowers individuals to take charge of their educational journey. These goals can range from acquiring new skills and exploring specific subjects to fostering a growth mindset.

Example Goals: Learning a new language, acquiring coding skills, or delving into a topic outside one's expertise are tangible examples of personal learning goals.

Integrating Technology for Learning

Online Learning Platforms: Accessible Education

The digital age has democratized education, making learning resources accessible to individuals worldwide. Online platforms offer courses, tutorials, and resources that cater to a diverse range of interests and skill levels.

Examples of Platforms: Khan Academy, Coursera, and YouTube provide a wealth of educational content on subjects ranging from science and mathematics to art and philosophy.

Podcasts and Educational Apps

Podcasts and educational apps offer convenient ways to learn on the go. Whether listening to experts discuss topics of interest or engaging in interactive learning experiences, these tools make knowledge acquisition flexible and enjoyable.

Example Apps: Duolingo for language learning, TED Talks for diverse perspectives, and educational podcasts on various subjects.

Cultivating a Reading Habit

Diverse Reading for Intellectual Growth

Reading is a timeless habit that stimulates intellectual growth and nurtures a love for learning. Lifelong learners embrace a diversity of genres, from fiction and non-fiction to literature and academic texts.

Example Reading Habits: Incorporating a mix of novels, biographies, scientific literature, and philosophical texts broadens intellectual horizons.

Reflective Reading Practices

Lifelong learners go beyond mere consumption; they engage in reflective reading practices. This involves analyzing and contemplating the material, fostering a deeper understanding and integration of knowledge.

Example Practices: Keeping a reading journal, discussing books with others, or participating in book clubs enhance the reflective aspect of reading.

Lifelong Learning in Professional Development

Continuous Skill Development

In a dynamic professional landscape, staying relevant and adaptable is crucial. Lifelong learners actively seek opportunities for continuous skill development, ensuring they remain competitive and valuable in their careers.

Example Skills: Learning new software, attending workshops, and pursuing certifications are practical examples of continuous skill development.

Networking and Collaborative Learning

Networking provides avenues for collaborative learning and knowledge exchange. Engaging with professionals in diverse fields fosters a community of learning, where insights and experiences are shared for mutual growth.

Example Networking Activities: Attending industry events, participating in online forums, and joining professional associations enhance collaborative learning.

The Role of Travel in Lifelong Learning

Cultural Immersion and Global Perspectives

Travel serves as a powerful catalyst for lifelong learning. Experiencing different cultures, traditions, and perspectives broadens one's worldview, fostering a deep appreciation for diversity.

Example Travel Practices: Engaging with locals, exploring historical sites, and immersing oneself in local customs contribute to cultural learning.

Educational Travel Experiences

Educational travel experiences, such as study abroad programs or learning-focused tours, provide structured opportunities for acquiring knowledge while exploring new environments.

Examples of Programs: Language immersion programs, historical tours, and educational cruises offer unique learning experiences.

Embracing Failure as a Learning Opportunity

Resilience Through Challenges

Lifelong learners view failures as opportunities for growth rather than setbacks. Embracing challenges, learning from mistakes, and adapting strategies contribute to resilience in the face of adversity.

Example Mindset: Rather than fearing failure, individuals with a growth mindset see challenges as chances to learn and improve.

Reflection on Setbacks

Reflective practices extend to setbacks and failures. Lifelong learners engage in introspection, identifying lessons learned from unsuccessful endeavors and applying those insights to future pursuits.

Example Reflection Questions: "What went wrong, and how can I improve?" or "What skills or knowledge gaps contributed to this setback?"

Real-Life Stories of Lifelong Learning

To illustrate the impact of lifelong learning habits, let's explore real-life stories of individuals who have embraced continuous learning throughout their lives.

Maria's Exploration of Coding in Midlife

Maria, in her mid-40s, decided to learn coding—an entirely new skill for her. Through online courses, coding bootcamps, and collaborative projects, Maria not only gained proficiency in coding languages but also transitioned into a new and fulfilling career in technology.

Raj's Multifaceted Learning Journey

Raj, a retiree, embarked on a multifaceted learning journey after retirement. He delved into subjects like astronomy, creative writing, and organic gardening. By combining online courses, local workshops, and hands-on experiences, Raj's retirement became a dynamic phase of continuous learning.

Conclusion: The Ever-Unfolding Tapestry of Learning

As Chapter 15 concludes, the essence of lifelong learning habits lies in their ability to ignite curiosity, foster personal growth, and contribute to a rich and fulfilling existence. Whether through formal education, self-directed learning, or experiential exploration, the journey of continuous learning is a lifelong adventure.

May the spirit of curiosity and the pursuit of knowledge continue to illuminate your path, enriching every step of your ongoing dance with the ever-unfolding tapestry of learning. As the final chapter concludes, may your journey be one of perpetual discovery and intellectual joy?

Closing Chapter: Embracing The Rhythm Of Habits Dear Readers,

As we approach the final act of our shared journey, let's unravel a profound lesson that echoes through the pages of the dance of habits—a lesson that transcends complexities and resonates deeply.

The Lesson: Your Habits Shape Your Destiny

In the intricate tapestry of life, habits are the threads weaving the patterns of our existence. Each small habit is a step in the dance, a note in the symphony that is your life. And the beautiful truth is this: you hold the choreography.

Lesson 1: Small Steps Lead to Great Journeys

Every significant journey begins with small steps. Habits are like those steps—simple actions that, when repeated, propel you forward. It's not about making colossal leaps; it's about taking consistent, small steps. Envision the dance floor of life as a vast expanse, and your habits as the rhythmic beats guiding your movement. With each small habit, you sway in the direction of your dreams.

Lesson 2: Choose Your Dance Partners Wisely

In the dance of habits, you are the choreographer, and your habits are your dance partners. Choose them wisely. opt for habits that resonate with your deepest aspirations, habits that harmonize with the melody of your values. Surround yourself with positive rhythms, and let your dance be a celebration of joy and fulfillment.

Lesson 3: Embrace the Dance of Imperfection

The dance floor of life is not a stage for perfection; it's a space for expression. Embrace the dance of imperfection, knowing that each misstep is an opportunity to learn and grow. Your habits are not meant to be flawless routines but evolving movements that shape your journey.

Lesson 4: Dance with Purpose

Your habits, like dance steps, gain meaning when infused with purpose. Let intention guide your movements. Why are you dancing? What rhythm do you wish to amplify? Align your habits with your purpose and watch as the dance becomes a powerful expression of your journey's meaning.

Inspiring Quotes to Illuminate Your Path

As we bid farewell, let the wisdom of others accompany you on the next steps of your dance:

"Your habits will shape your future. Choose them wisely." - Unknown

"Dance like no one is watching, and let your habits be the rhythm of your joy."

"In the dance of life, every habit is a step towards destiny." - Anonymous

"Small steps, big impact. Your habits create the dance of your life."

"Life is a dance, and your habits are the music that guides your steps."

Closing Notes: Shaping Your Destiny

In the dance of habits, you are not a mere spectator; you are the dancer, the choreographer, and the composer of your destiny. As you navigate the dance floor of life, remember: your habits are the brushstrokes on the canvas of your existence.

May your dance be vibrant, purposeful, and filled with the joy of positive habits. The stage is yours, the music is playing, and the dance is an ever-unfolding masterpiece.

Sincerely,

Shahnawaz

Writer, Choreographer of Life's Dance, and Fellow Traveler in the Symphony of Habits

www.ingramcontent.com/pod-product-compliance
Lightning Source LLC
LaVergne TN
LVHW021200160826
845679LV00024B/2186

9798892771337